Teaching the Heart to Sing

To Sarah —
With love & reverence —
Julie Redstone

Dear Friends,

If you have felt inspired by the material in this book and would like to receive our catalog of tapes by Julie Redstone, or if you would like to be notified of a workshop being offered by her in your area, please print your name and address clearly on the other side of this card.

If you would like to know about other Uni-Sun publications and to be put on Uni-Sun's mailing list, please indicate this as well.

Julie welcomes your feelings and reactions to the material presented in this book, and asks you to share them in the space below or in a letter.

Yours in Light,
THE AMHERST CENTER FOR HEALING

———— Please send me your catalog of tapes by Julie Redstone, and let me know about workshops being offered by her in my area.

———— I am interested in having Julie come to my area to do a workshop and would be willing to arrange this.

———— Please put my name on Uni-Sun's mailing list and let me know about other Uni-Sun books and products.

JULIE REDSTONE
AMHERST CENTER FOR HEALING
PO BOX 947
AMHERST, MA. 01004-0947

᭛ The Old Vicarage, Hawkesbury, Badminton, Avon, GL9 1BW ᭛

FROM Sir George Trevelyan
A commentary on **Teaching the Heart to Sing**

This is a lovely book, an inspired book, through which the wisdom flows like crystal fresh water from a spring. It was sent to me when other matters pressed and I had little time, but grudgingly I opened after a long day's journeying. And having started I could not put the book down but read deep into the night, slept a little and on waking took it up again and finished it.

Julie Redstone has given us a wonderful affirmation of the Spirit as the force at work in world transformation, God as Life wherever we can apprehend it, Love as that aspect of the Creator which IS the Living Christ everywhere, the reality of the Angelic Kingdom, and the wonder of realization that the Higher World speaks within our own thinking.

This is the great turn-about in the centre of our consciousness, the vital phenomenon of our time, put in this book in terms anyone with an open mind can understand. The true New Age Vision must recognize that we human beings are each a divine droplet, eternal and imperishable, and that evolution on the Planet has, in our generation, reached the point of awakening to our true destiny. Teach the Heart to Sing, indeed!

This is a message of joy. This light-filled book is channelled by one who has experienced illumination.

This is a message of joy. In an age full of forboding and fear, we discover the reality of the Worlds of Spirit and the immediate Divine Presence surrounding and transfusing our lives. The whole of Eternity is ours for the true adventure in self-development into the Living Whole, which is the Light and Love of God and His Angels.

I urge you to read this book—and rejoice.

Sir George Trevelyan
April 1989

TEACHING THE HEART TO SING:

A Guide To Shifting Consciousness At The Dawn Of A New Age

Julie Redstone, Ph.D.

Uni★Sun

Kansas City

Uni★Sun
P.O. Box 25421
Kansas City, MO 64119

This book is manufactured in the United States of America. Distribution by The Talman Company:

The Talman Co.
150 Fifth Avenue
New York, NY 10011

Library of Congress Cataloging-in-Publication Data

Redstone, Julie.
    Teaching the heart to sing.

    1. Spirit writings. 2. Spiritual life. I. Title.
BF1290.R43 1989   133.9'3   88-51920
ISBN 0-912949-28-7

Cover photo by Jim Gipe
Back cover photo by Mark Kosarick
Cover Design by Daniel, Richter & Rood.
Book design by Pat Huyett

A
Uni★Sun
BOOK

Let Thy wish become my desire,
Let Thy will become my deed,
Let Thy word become my speech, Beloved,
And Thy love become my creed.

—A Sufi Song

TEACHING THE HEART TO SING:

*A Guide To Shifting Consciousness
At The Dawn Of A New Age.*

Part III. LOVE

Part IV. TRANSFORMATION

Dedication

To the indwelling Spirit—She who carries me in her arms to the place in the stars that is my Home—the Divine Mother, To Archangel Michael, giver of strength, of clarity, and of the sword of discrimination. Above all, that holy messenger who has blessed me with his love and with a sense of holy purpose.

To the Spirit that moves upon the face of the waters—Whose face I seek behind all forms, and Whom I shall adore forever.

Foreword

This is a work brought into manifestation by we of the angelic realm—the collective Mind of the Archangels Michael, Gabriel, Raphael, and Uriel, and the superconscious mind of one who has been willing to receive our message and act as our translator and co-creator. We bring to the Earth at this time many messages of hope and of new vision, that those who have waited for so long for a sign of the reality of the celestial hierarchies may know that we are indeed real, and intently concerned with the growth and development of the Earth. Our message is broadcast to all who would receive it and we invite each heart that reads these words to open more fully to the spiritual reality that is being revealed.

For you, Beloveds, are the ones for whom we have waited throughout time, till that day upon which you would awaken to the truth of your inner being—of your Divine nature. That time of waiting is coming to an end and we joyously anticipate the moment in which we will begin our journey together in creating light and life. A journey beyond the wildest dreams of possibility for many of you, yet one which will indeed be undertaken by all.

We come to you in peace and love, and offer you our deepest blessings, Beloveds, for this journey is about to begin.

Introduction

This book was written in one month, between October 14th and November 14th 1987, with no conscious planning or prior expectation on my part. It is given here exactly as received, with no revisions except in grammar, and in the organization of chapters to provide a clearer presentation. It began with my sitting down at the typewriter on that first day and thinking to myself: "I think I'll write a book called *Teaching the Heart to Sing.*" Though words similar to this, (ie. "you are to teach others to sing") had come to me as night-time guidance several times during the previous week, I had no idea material for a book would present itself.

Impulsively and without conscious thought that first morning I wrote out a Table of Contents after the title, then sat down, closed my eyes, and waited for the first chapter to appear. Only after the first chapter had been written, and the second flowed out with equal ease, as did the third and fourth, did I begin to believe that this book already existed within me, and within the collective Mind that I appeared to be tapping into—the Mind of the Archangels.

On October 15th, just after beginning to write, I asked for guidance and was told that the Archangels Michael, Raphael, Gabriel, and Uriel were co- authoring this book with my Higher Self, but it was not until after the completion of the book on November 15th, that the actual process of beginning was made clearer to me:

The determination to begin this book came not from a place of conscious motivation, but rather from the guid-

ance and instruction of the Higher Self. At the level of Oneness, all purposes share one common purpose and blend with the individual soul purpose for a particular incarnation. There is no separation between your motives for writing this, and our motives for having it written by you.

Your sincere desire to help others and to be an instrument for their learning was highly prized by those who wish to teach the truths of the One Beloved, and so it is with a synchronicity of intention that this work was undertaken, to fully manifest both your goals and ours, yours as a communicator and conveyor of truth, and ours as would—be guides to humanity about to take wing. . . .

Your devotion to the cause of truth is felt by those about you, and does not go unnoticed by we of the angelic realm either. For truth is a precious jewel, given to those who seek to know, and it shines like a star within the darkness of confusion and unclarity...

Though I recognized this as true, the possiblity of my channeling material like this, either for clients or in printed form would have been inconceivable just two years ago.

My career as a clinical psychologist had taken a drastic turn in 1982 when a sudden spiritual awakening brought me into startling awareness of another reality—a world more real than the one I thought I lived in—the world of spiritual Truth. Simultaneously with that opening, I began to channel healing energy. As that process began I continued to hold onto the identity I had grown up with, and it took two full years before I could acknowledge to myself that I had become a "healer." Then one year later I was suddenly no longer just a healer, but had begun to speak on spiritual themes in public and had become a teacher and lecturer.

The change which completing this writing has produced within me is of a similar radical nature. I have now to understand that I am learning to open to the higher Truth of the Archangels who guide humanity, and that I am being guided in my work and in my writing by these Beings.

Out of this process of change and growth in learning to trust Spirit has come many gifts. Strength, compassion, and love for all beings expand within me as I daily surrender to the inner Light—the voice of my Higher Self. Therefore it is with a sense of gratitude and of blessedness that I offer this book to others—an offering from the higher realms of Truth and Love, and from my own heart's deep yearning to serve the Divine Light within all. Accept this with my love and the love of the angelic realm, to honor the beautiful Divine beings that you are.

Julie Redstone
December 24, 1987

PART I: *Awakening*

We are discovering, as we let go of the old identities, that we are not an "I" in any sense that we had conceived of ourselves, but rather a pulsating point of light forever intertwined with all other points of light, forever held in the Mind of God that holds in Love the vastness of this Universe.

Chapter 1

An Awakening into Being

Beloveds, a great awakening is taking place on our
planet. We are finding ourselves casting off the con-
straints of old identities and being drawn toward the realization of nameless and unknown parts of ourselves. For it
is a time of awakening to spiritual life—to a sense of participation in the cosmos. And indeed, we are each cosmic citizens who by birthright have a connection and involvement with everything that takes place throughout the Universe. We are *children* of the Universe, and everywhere we
are leaving behind the limitations of parochialism in order
to more fully realize our universality.

On one level it is the child within that is being born, the
child that lives in a state of awe and wonder, surprised at
the newness of each moment, each color, each sound—
taking nothing for granted, revelling in the sparkling
elasticity that is life—formless, brilliant, and unknowable.
And it is the child within that is learning to trust this state
of splendor that it is discovering—to trust the newness and
the unnameability, leaving behind the more adult concepts
and labels that we have given ourselves in order to answer
the question: "Who am I?"

We are discovering, as we let go of the old identities,
that we are not an "I" in any sense that we had conceived

of ourselves, but rather a pulsating point of light forever intertwined with all other points of light, forever held in the Mind of God that holds in Love the vastness of this Universe. As we awaken we are forced to question our safety, for security, as we have known it, is gone forever. And what is there in its place is the everpresent current that animates our being, that flows through us at all times and speaks to us of who we are. Do we have the ears yet to hear this?

Some of us hesitate in fear before the power of this nameless force which blows through our lives—this new energy which asks that we release all holding onto "me" and "mine"; at times we lack the courage to do so. And yet, it is being done through us, as well as by us. Not a movement that the conscious mind or "ego" dictates, for the conscious mind is bound by constructions of reality whose purpose is to create a sense of control over life and over others—to defend and protect us from the un- foreseen circumstances of life which we feared. Since this fear is the foundation upon which the ego developed, it cannot now become the voice of trust for us as we awaken.

Only the indwelling Spirit as it speaks to us of the greater life to which we are being called, can begin to in- still within each one of us that trust which is beyond mea- sure. For it is trust in the order of the Universe and in the rightness of all things. Beyond measure and beyond logic—for this degree of trust cannot be based on the *logic* of ordinary vision, which sees that the world as we know it does not make sense, is often cruel, unjust, and filled with fear and longing. The trust we seek requires more than or- dinary perception. It requires the presence of a miracle within us—a miracle of faith on which to build a newly created life.

We are being called, each and every one of us to this new life. And as we hear this call, we realize that what we are being called to is the joy of being asked to sing our own song in the concert of celestial beings. For indeed, each one of us has a song to sing that is truly our own, and only by becoming one with the emerging truth within us do we allow ourselves to become part of the celestial chorus.

It has been said that humankind are fallen angels. That once united with the celestial choirs and the Light and Love pervading the Universe, we are now submerged in limited thinking, and have become shadows of our real selves. Now it is important to know that we are not fallen angels. Only in the sense of having forgotten our true heritage have we fallen from Grace. There is no sin involved in this, other than the sin of leaving the state of complete and total harmony with all that is, which is our natural birthright. Mankind and womankind have been, are, and will be greater than the angels as we awaken to our true being. For the angelic kingdom has never left the state of oneness to enter the state of duality that humans live in, and therefore has yet to experience the full individualization of God-consciousness to which each of us is being born.

We, humankind, have the honor to have chosen, and to have been chosen, to move through the sphere of duality, in order to fully embody the consciousness of God within form. I and you and all our brothers and sisters of the Earth are beautiful Divine images, held securely in the Mind of God. And it is our destiny to realize in full consciousness the image which forms the ground of our individuality, and of our being.

So let the light be seen within us. There is nothing we need do anymore to hide from ourselves or from others. The era of living according to the human standard of appearance and approval is giving way to something greater. Our mission and our destiny, yes, each of us individually, is to open our hearts to the greater being-ness flowing through us, calling us more and more imperatively to become our true selves. For it is only by becoming our true selves that we allow God to become one with us, and to pervade the physical realm with the holiness of spiritual life. We are being called to this task. It is our choice to determine how fearless we may be in accepting our greatness.

The world is already changing according to this greater concept of the meaning of life. Although vast areas of the Earth are still embedded in and resonating with patterns of fear and selfishness, change is increasingly in the air. It is all around us. And we breathe it in with each breath that we take; we nourish our bodies with it and give life to our spiritual selves.

Selfishness may not disappear from the Earth before the transformation is complete. And there will be some who will choose to continue their learning of self-and-God-realization on other planes of existence. But for the Earth the emerging pattern is clear: we are to awaken to the glory of knowing that we are here to manifest and embody peace, love, and the opening of the channel to the divinity within us.

Let God's face appear to all children of Earth, that what has been spoken of as the Kingdom of Heaven may bring its fulfilling presence into the lives of all who wait eagerly for it.

PAX

. . . it is the time for the progressive revelation of the power of Love, and all help is given to those who have cast off fear sufficiently to allow something new, even something half-understood, to enter their awareness.

Chapter 2

The Return of the Christ

B eloveds, we have come to a point in our history where it may be known that the power to control life, that it may bring us what we wish and long for—the only power that is real—is the power of Love. For when we love, we automatically place ourselves in harmony with the flow of the Universe—that which binds all things to each other—people, planets, stars, galaxies. That which brings all into relationship is the force of Love.

Therefore, when we seek to master more fully the life that we are entrusted with, and the circumstances that are before us, it is important for us to remember that we are as Gods here on the Earth, and have only to attune ourselves to the highest reaches of thought—to the One force pervading the Universe—in order to tap into the universal energy that is already present within us and around us.

What does this mean in practice? It means that we awaken the Christ within us through our willingness to let go of all motives that are not grounded in love; to release all patterns of thought that do not emerge from the matrix of the loving universal Spirit of whom we are a part. This is what brings into the present reality the Christ, and this is what is needed now in order to master and harmonize the chaotic flow of current world events.

There is no alternative to this for our planet and for us as individuals. A spiritual path which does not come back to this central point of manifesting the Christ within leaves that being who follows it with the prospect of less than God-consciousness.

When we consider the "wayshowers" that have come to our world as teachers and spritual guides, we recognize in the patterning of their lives the everpresent manifestation of Love. Whether they be gurus, or monks, or ordinary people living within cities, the single most important feature of one who would incarante the Christ-consciousness is the willingness to love all that is.

Jesus came to the Earth to demonstrate this truth and has lived and will live for all time within our hearts as a model and lodestar to which we may bring our thoughts, time and time again. To become the Christ, we must live a life built on love as the dominant motif, letting go of the sense of embarrassment, even of humiliation, that still occurs within some of us as we move within a world that does not yet accept the presence of Love as a power. It is but a matter of time before we of this planet realize that all forms of power, other than the power of Love will fail, for they are built not of Spirit but of ego. And to anchor the Christ consciousness within the Earth is not a choice that an individual can choose *not* to make. For the Earth itself is about to fully embody the Christ-light. And we of the Earth must either learn to move with this change, or determine to continue our learning in other spheres. There is no such thing as death and therefore souls that will not make the change in synchronicity with the Earth's leap will not be punished. But they will also not be allowed to prevent the Earth and those beings who continue their lives upon it from moving forward at their own evolutionary tempo.

Some of us will want to know what will be gained in exchange for that which is given up as a basis for human action: they will not be convinced of the power of love to bring into manifestation all that is needed and all that is wished for. These skeptical ones are present in the world all around us and must be gently led into trust and realization. Opening the heart to love is a process that moves in concert with the movement of the spheres. The planets themselves, at this time in our history, are raying benevolent energy toward the Earth, helping her on her way into greater realization. And countless beings throughout the Universe—the Brotherhood of guides and Master teachers, the Great Ones from other galactic systems, the angels and Archangels, all are arrayed on the side of light bursting into Love upon this planet. All stand waiting to help each individual to experience any opportunity to open to the meaning of love.

No experience is wasted; none goes unnoticed. If there is a possiblity for a being to open the smallest chink in his or her armor of defenses to let in more light, these guides and helpers who are ever watchful over their precious Earthchild will help and assist that one into greater recognition of love and unity. *For it is the time for the progressive revelation of the power of Love, and all help is given to those who have cast off fear sufficiently to allow something new, even something half-understood, to enter their awareness.*

The Christ returns. And with this magnificent presence comes into the physical plane the presence of teachers and guides in physical form in far greater number. Those who have been teachers and leaders in other cycles in the past are becoming empowered by that same loving force that moves through each of us, to become even more powerful in their desire to spread the word of Love. It has been said that those who are intelligent will become wise, those who are wise will become Masters, and those who are Masters will become one with the One. All life-forms upon the Earth today are moving forward in their evolution at an accelerated rate as the Christ energy, projected from the center of the galaxy and from the Mind of God, permeates the Earth's atmosphere to a greater and greater degree.

And what of those who cannot open to this vibration? That is a question that keeps coming up, often asked out of fear or a sense of personal inadequacy, rather than a sense of strength and hope. It is not possible to know, even now, when so many are powerfully affected by the changing energies, who will open and who will not. The smallest incident may be the beginning of a new perception of reality for us. For it is not taking place within the conscious mind, this transformation, but rather within our greater consciousness—our true relationship with life. And so the conscious mind may remain quite skeptical, even closed to love and truth, while the larger consciousness absorbs the new energy that is about. Until one day a book falls into our hands that is life-changing, or a friend makes a remark that starts us thinking, or relationships that we have felt quite sure about suddenly begin to look different, and demand to be evaluated differently— these are not the result of a conscious thought process but rather of a shift in awareness which is taking place internally and externally.

Understand this: We are forever inextricably connected with the Earth and with the cosmos. And as the Earth changes in her vibration and her awareness, it must be that all beings that are part of her physical and vibratory body change with her. There is no standing apart from this process.

PAX

The resurrection brings to each child of God not only his or her own path to the Holy of Holies, but unites in common bond all creatures great and small, all kingdoms high and low, that God may know His dwelling place among all of creation.

Chapter 3

The Message of the Christ

Beloveds, I Am the Resurrection and the Light, the dawning of a new day that all will behold, keeping the promises of old now for those who have waited without ceasing to pray for My coming. I come before you to annoint you with the waters of Life, to bring you to the fountain from which all life flows—the fountain of eternal oneness.

These words that I impart to you this day shall pierce the skin of the hardest of hearts and shall resound from the mountain tops. They shall overturn cities and bring the mighty into a state of helplessness. For they are the words of victory of Light over darkness and of hope over despair. This civilization has for too long been victim of the pride and prejudices of the minority who have sought to maintain power, not for the sake of truth, but for the sake of ego. This sword of power shall now be returned to the dwelling place of love where it has forever belonged, and power and love shall be united always. My energy, which begins to pass through you and among you, shall distinguish between the righteous and the unjust, the godly and the god-less. In the days to come it shall penetrate to the very depths of individual being as it penetrates to the core of the Earth.

I AM the Resurrection and the Light. I sweep all before me in the tide of change, for change will come, welcomed or not. And I ask, for the sake of Him whom you have called the Redeemer, that each one of you be willing to bear the cross with Him—the cross of matter—and accept the responsiblity for sanctifying your life, that the sacred promise you made upon entering this beautiful and holy Earth sphere may be kept. This was the promise to bear witness to the sanctity of matter and form, and to make sacred and holy all actions and thoughts, that all might offer a hymn of praise to God.

The resurrection brings to each child of God not only his or her own path to the Holy of Holies, but unites in common bond all creatures great and small, all kingdoms high and low, that God may know His dwelling place among all of creation.

Now is the time, Beloveds, for you to realize that the resurrection is already beginning in your midst. For those of you who are reclaiming your right to eternal life, it has begun, and shall continue until there are no empty places at the Lord's table. Until all recognize their common need to dine on the same spiritual food.

In one sense there is no hurry, for there is all of eternity waiting to receive you. Yet there is a need for those who would quicken the pace of personal and planetary history to become in word and in deed disciples of the Lord. The energy that is moving through all will move all that blocks it, for that is the nature of spiritual evolution. Yet those willing beings whose hearts flow with the love of Spirit may unblock this energy more quickly, in order that the many may feel less pain as the channel to Spirit opens.

The time of separation is ending. We are no longer separated from you: we in Spirit and you in physical bodies. We are one in essence and one in purpose. And you too are no longer to be separated from one another. For the effect of each choice that you make now has consequences far beyond any that you might imagine. For good or for evil your every thought ripples out into the Universe to create an atmo-

sphere in which other beings live and flourish or go hungry. Be aware therefore, dear ones, that the powerful incoming energies of the Christ activate to an even greater degree than before the power of your thoughts. For good or for evil. There is more power to be put to the use of evolution and movement into the future, or to the purpose of spreading fear and destruction. Be aware.

Be aware that you each individually carry the key which unlocks the door of your personal and planetary future. The distant outcome cannot be changed, for that has been determined by God. But the specific sequence of events which are initiated by the Christ energies is activated by every thought and every word spoken by every son and daughter of God. There is no escape from this responsibility. So be forewarned and learn to live with greater love. For this is the message of the Christ and of the resurrection. That he who lives by the sword shall die by the sword by remaining within the fixed belief in the reality of physical death. While he who lives according to the dictates of love shall expand into the consciousness of oneness with all Love—the Divine Father-Mother Spirit and Creator of the Universe.

I AM the resurrection and the Light. Come unto me and rest your weary hearts, for My energy moves among you now, and empowers you to reach greater heights and take broader steps than you would have dared to before. Know that you are not alone, and that this truth will become more and more apparent to you. The very atoms of the Universe are supporting you on your journey home. The physical substance of your very physical world is vibrating at a higher rate than what you have been accustomed to, and is intensifying the speed of your growth into awareness of the only true reality—your spiritual being.

It is not a time for fear, Beloveds, but for joy. For each of you is being assisted in every way possible to open the doors to that selfhood which has been given to you as a gift—that self which longs to sing its own song and join the celestial harmonies. Allow the energy of the Christ—that which proclaims itself: I AM THAT I AM—to dwell within the forms of your life, that each of you individually and all of you together may realize the fullness of being that has always been yours, and that now awaits your acceptance of it.

PAX

In the times ahead, this above all will be asked of us—willing surrender to the experience of the moment. A willingness to allow what is, within ourselves and outside of ourselves, to be.

Chapter 4

The Restoration of the Kingdom

B eloveds, there is no limit to the creative power of the energy presently entering the Earth's atmosphere. It may be thought of as a fine dust invisibly falling on all things, or as a powerful laser beam penetrating the heart of even the most opaque object. This energy emitted from the spiritual core of the galaxy and circulating throughout the entire solar system, is more refined and of a higher frequency of vibration than any that the Earth has yet beheld. On one level it may be said to carry the vibration of the Christ-consciousness, for this is its purpose: to create an intimate knowledge of the fact that the sons and daughters of the Universe and the Father-Mother Spirit are one. Yet on another level, the energy consists simply of rays of light inaccessible to ordinary vision, which create in the human being the ability to *see* more clearly.

As this light descends, it becomes ever more important for us to consider what it is that we wish to see, and what it is that we are *willing* to see. For the light will reveal whatever it is that the heart and mind are focused on. It will illuminate more clearly and with greater intensity than before anything which falls within its beam.

Just as the sunlight does not discriminate in its downward flow between the thief and the saint, but falls equally

27

upon all, so too will the rays of God's increasing illumination make visible that which has been hidden. For the intensifying light is a form of energy that we are now to incorporate into our bodies—yes, even into the cellular level of our physical bodies, and into the planetary body as well. Its sacred purpose is to raise the level of our spiritual awareness—to bring all beings into harmonious attunement with one another and with the Spirit of the Universe.

Therefore dear ones, it is the task of each and every one of us to bring into this light, with courage, faith, and a desire to surrender, all that is hidden within us. And for each one what that means will differ. For it is not just that which pertains to this life-cycle that we are speaking of, but rather that which has been kept in semi-consciousness, undisturbed, throughout the entire re-incarnational cycle that must now be transmuted.

Remember that each of us, from the beginning of time as we conceive it, has been moving along the path of our soul's choosing toward a divinely appointed goal. Whether conscious of this or not, we are each on the pathway home. Yet what remains for us as we move forward is the clearing away of the debris from past lives and from this present life—those areas of density and darkness which block the full passage of the light of Spirit into the inner chamber of the heart where the threefold flame of the I AM Presence dwells.

It is with compassion for the self and with a desire for greater understanding that each must surrender his darkness to the Light. In this process, whatever lives within us as the residue of pain, fear, doubt, anger, or despair, must become fully conscious. This is the true meaning and context of the word "release"—a word that will assume greater and greater importance in our minds and hearts as the energies of purificiation intensify on the Earth plane. To *release* the darkness within us to the Light we must allow it to become fully conscious, to recognize it fully as our own, and yet to not identify with it or become submerged by it. It must be seen as a cloud or a mist that we are passing through for a time. As we travel forward in faith through this mist, we must hold firmly to the idea that the loss of greater vision is only a transient event within space and time, and that the darkness we must pass through will open our consciousness to the greater reality which lies beyond.

Beloveds, the time will come when we shall feel behind the movement of every leaf blown in the wind, behind every face sullen with age or worry, and behind every task that seems gargantuan and overwhelming, the kiss of the Divine breath, blowing through the Universe, penetrating all creation with its Spirit and power. For it is not within *our* power to create or alter a single thread of the fabric which God has woven into the story of the evolution of matter: *that* is given, and is gifted to us. It is within our power only to withhold or release those obstacles to greater awareness which prevent us from sensing this Divine breath and from seeing this exquisite light dancing eternally within and around each form.

For those who accept and cling to the idea that the material plane exists unto itself, there is no dancing. For they see a world separated from the world of meaning, governed only by laws pertaining to physical matter, understood only by movements of the rational mind. The Universe is not and has never been a physical artifact. Now and always it is inseparable from the spiritual meaning which has created it and which keeps it unfolding in Light. *There is no leaf that blows in the breeze that does not speak with a voice of greater truth than we can hear.* The movement of the leaf is a living metaphor for us—a symbol of the life-force expressing itself through form—the form, surrendering to the life-force from which it gains its meaning.

What history has created as a concept of evolution—

which assigns meaning to a certain sequence of events, and out of this definition creates a philosophy of life—is no more the truth about reality than that the event of the leaf's blossoming and then falling is the truth about that leaf. The history of the leaf's arrival into and abandonment of its physical form is filled with interest and even wonder for us, but it does not approach the wonder of what the leaf sings of: life endlessly the creator of form—form endlessly the lover and the beloved of life. This is what the leaf and the breeze speak of. And also, of the importance of willing surrender, of non-resistance to what is.

In the times ahead, this above all will be asked of us— willingness to surrender to the experience of the moment. A willingness to allow what is within ourselves and outside of ourselves to be. Within each of us there are pools and reservoirs of fear and mistrust—of ourselves, of others, and of God, that must come to light before the Kingdom itself can be revealed. These pools and eddies of mistrust have been kept from the current of life because of our fear of consciousness. Now these dark corners of our being are to be swept clean by the Christ energy, that we may know the fullness of the Divine beings that we are. It is not so much a stepping forward in courage that must be taken, although this is helpful. It is more a step of opening the arms, of embracing, of allowing, of permission—that what is, shall be—a reflection of God. This faith can transform the experience of pain by creating a universal context for it, so that we will no longer need to fear pain, or to blame ourselves or others for it. Rather, we will see pain as the illumination of inner or outer darkness, by the light-rays of Divine being.

Can you imagine, dear ones, what the world would be like if people did not fear pain, but rather trusted its goodness? Can you imagine what the experience of terminal illness or any other chronic disease would be like, if pain were seen merely as a transitional phase, a state like a mist that one passes through, in order to arrive at the light on the other side of the mist? We would ask for the support and compassion of those who love us to help us navigate through this mist, but we would not need to harden ourselves to it, or judge ourselves harshly for having brought this pain upon ourselves, or blame our lives or a particular relationship for bringing us into pain.

Pain, dear ones, is a *transmutative element*—that which is experienced as negative, but which *inevitably* brings us into a more positive alignment with life, and with a deeper level of our being. This is not a reason to *seek* pain as a learning tool, for such desire is not within the human personality. But rather to receive it in gentleness, as a guide and as a beacon toward growth in an area that is yet to be determined.

The signal function of pain is still necessary for most of us during this stage of our spritual evolution. There will be a time in the future, however, when pain will not be a necessary learning device—when we have experienced our oneness with our Divine source. Yet pain at this time is necessary to circumvent the obstacles that we have erected in our consciousness of reality. It brings into our lives the necessity of rethinking and re- evaluating our most heartfelt thoughts, values, and priorities. And so as the light of God's illumination penetrates our hearts more and more, we may expect some pain to reveal its presence to us. And it will be a sign to us that we are being brought back home. For in this process, we are indeed being offered the outstretched arm of the Divine Mother, still unseen, who lifts us out of our unconscious selves, out of the fear and denial that we have accepted as limiting ideas, into the light of awareness, of knowledge, and of new birth.

As we experience this birth, we shall see the Kingdom of Heaven appear upon the face of the Earth where it has always been. And we shall know why we have not had the eyes to see it. For to see the spiritual light and life around us, we must see with the clear vision of our inner light, the clear heart of our inner knowing, and the clear mind of our inner truth. When we arrive at this state of clarity, through purification and a desire to be revealed to ourselves, then we shall see the Kingdom restored upon the Earth.

PAX

This is what must be understood about doubt: that it is the fertile ground for the creation of faith. That those who struggle with doubt are struggling to find truth and God within themselves at a deeper level than many who, on the surface, seem to have been given a gift of faith.

Chapter 5

The Sanctuary of Doubt

Beloveds, we are often disposed to wish that we could live with more faith, for faith brings peace and an end to our relentless worrying. Yet it is in the state of *doubt* that we need to seek the real answer to our prayers, for this is where the work of surrender needs to be done. Faith is a place of arrival—it is home. Doubt is a place of holiness and of learning on our way. It is a resting place.

How is it possible to rest within doubt, we ask, for doubt for most produces fear and discomfort. This is a difficult question to answer, for we must re-conceive all that we have thought about what it means to work and what it means to rest. Perhaps we might consider that to rest might be defined as being in a place of regrouping—of regaining our strength so that we may go on later. Doubt in this context, might be viewed as a bootcamp at the lowest level of a mountain climb from which we ascend to the peak. It is a place from which we view the ascent and the peak, and from which we travel forth in order to make the climb. In this sense, we must redefine the relationship between doubt and faith—doubt being the lowest level of a path that leads inevitably to faith.

To understand the true nature of doubt, we need to learn to see through the eyes of a Master like Jesus, who could bring his own light to the doubtful and the faithless and transform them. We need to recall how often his presence had this effect on those who initially did not accept his teachings. Consider that Jesus did not ask those whom he healed to assert or demonstrate their faith *before* he performed his healings. It is those who came from a background of disbelief and denial who were often healed. What we must see is that when Jesus proclaimed, "Go now, your faith has made you whole," he was describing a *process* achieved through the interaction of doubt with Light, his Light, which in the presence of the individual's *desire to believe* transformed doubt into faith. They were made whole by their desire to find faith within themselves.

This is what must be understood about doubt—that it is the fertile ground for the creation of faith. That those who struggle with doubt are struggling to find truth and God within themselves at a deeper level than many who on the surface seem to have been given a gift of faith.

Let us recognize that there is no experience more threatening to individuals than to doubt the truth of what they most deeply believe in—to doubt their most securely held values. And so it is often difficult to rest in doubt. Yet this is precisely what must be done to penetrate to a *deeper* level of truth within ourselves.

As the Light illuminates the darkness of our soul's longing we will not be able to say any longer, "I believe this, I do not believe this." Increasingly we will say, "I do not know what I believe." And we will mean by this that we are travelling through a land of un-knowing where truth becomes a progressive revelation in the midst of doubt, while we trust that we will be led further. There are wonderful guides who have gone before us into this land of unknowing, people like Thomas Merton, T.S. Eliot,

Thoreau, and many of the Hindu sages and saints of all ages. And yet even with guidance and a lighted path, we will each still experience the darkness and fear that doubt produces, until we feel and see the light *within ourselves* that will illuminate the darkness around us forever. No other can do this for us. It is part of God's chosen plan for creation and of our individual soul's plan for the realization of the Spirit within, that we travel through the terrain of doubt into faith, that our Spirit may soar in its quest for the heights of Truth and oneness with God.

Remember that it is not a matter of being "bad" that causes us to doubt; it is a matter of being human. As long as we are embedded in our consciousness in perceiving a world of duality, we will be dealing with doubt. For the basis of doubt is the perceived separation of man from God, of good from evil, and of pleasure from pain. Doubt reflects the state of our consciousness of oneness with the Creator. It is a sacred state, a transmutative state, which imperceptibly leads us into faith.

Much of contemporary thought, particularly in the area of quantum physics, is changing even now our concepts of a dualistic universe with separate, discrete objects in it. And this will be increasingly true as our attention is brought more and more, through different scientific and artistic discoveries, to the vision of ourselves and all life as unified within an interdependent field of action and reaction. As we come to accept this vision, we will have an easier time realizing that doubt does not stand apart from faith, nor pain from pleasure, nor good from evil, but rather that they define each other, and in a sense have produced each other in the cycles of time, as the rhythmic alternation of energy throughout history has swung from one point to another along every value-continuum.

Yet this very pattern of alternation between doubt and faith is what is about to change, as humanity takes its first steps into the New Age. For the energy of the Christ consciousness is an energy that defines within us a new awareness—one in which concepts and judgments regarding physical reality are released, as we increasingly see the physical as a shadow and mirror of an underlying spiritual Truth. In the Light of the Christ, both doubt and faith are replaced by *knowing* (gnosis) the reality of God. Pain and pleasure are replaced by *seeing* the true meaning of events. Thus, a new consciousness of oneself emerges—of a self no longer alone but connected through the *experienced reality* of Spirit.

We are now at a point of needing to prepare the way within ourselves for this transition into knowing. At present we are still doubtful about God, about spiritual Truth, and about ourselves. And we are looking for insight to bring us out of this state of discomfort. In our searching, we often feel like children in a foreign land without parents or guides, seeking a sign of reassurance that all is well and that we will find our way home to a place of greater security.

The challenge of the present moment is to remain in this state of doubt and strangeness, without prematurely removing ourselves from it through denial or flight. We must be able to wait within this state of mind, to rest within it until the light of truth dawns within our minds and the outstretched hand of the Divine Mother points the way home. Paradoxically, as we wait for faith to appear to us, we are *being* faith-full to ourselves and to the emerging state of truth within us. We are trusting the path of consciousness itself to lead us into greater light. Without so naming it, within the land of doubt we are recognizing and reclaiming our indwelling divinity.

We may see a paradigm for this our present journey in the story of Moses and the Jewish people as they fled from Egypt and crossed the Sinai Desert. To walk, unseeing, to a land they knew not, led by an inner vision that commanded them to give up all claims to knowing—this was a test of faith and of the willingness to rest in doubt. And as the Bible reveals, many were not able to do this, but rather chose to end the state of uncertainty by deciding that God was not leading them and that the vision of Moses could not be trusted. Thus, a golden calf was created to symbolize the end of doubt and of surrender to the unknown and the creation of a new certainty. That man would now worship what he chose—the image of God that would offer the greatest material reward. And that man, not the Unknowable would once again resume control of his own life.

Beloveds, this story reflects a tendency still with us: to foreclose the state of doubt by a decision to seize control of life, even if this decison means sacrificing our sense of "rightness." We must be compassionate toward ourselves as this desire surfaces within us, for the desire to control our life is stronger than any other, *except* the desire for truth, spiritual meaning, and love. Until this desire for spiritual truth evolves within our being at some point in our soul's evolution, the desire for truth and love and the ego's desire for control of life will be in conflict with each other, for they are built on different premises. When this point of evolution is reached, however, the search for faith *through* the experience of doubt, becomes the primary search of the human being.

Before this point is reached there is much rejoicing over the "golden calf," much relief at the sense of freedom found at not having to surrender before the Most High, and pride at being able to run the show oneself. That this is an illusion has not yet penetrated the consciousness, and so is not felt as a loss. But by the point of spiritual advancement where doubt is experienced as a *primary emotion* in our lives, it becomes not merely a psychological perception experienced on the emotional level, but rather part of a spiritual transition which is of monumental proportions.

This is the transition that large groups of people will be

coming to at this point in our human history. For this sacred time within our present historical drama involves above all, the transition from fear and doubt to a new consciousness of the basis for faith.

PAX

There is no task more sacred for us at this time than the task of discovering the truth of our individuality within form, and our sameness in Spirit. In rediscovering this truth, we regain the sense of our own uniqueness and the uniquenss of all other individuals, in fact all other life-forms.

Chapter 6

The Sacred Boundary

Beloveds, we have come to a point in human history where it is necessary to reflect upon our lives as individuals in pursuit of specific goals—to consider both the meaning and purpose of our individuality, and the source and significance of the goals we are seeking. Many of us have set goals for ourselves from the time we were children, goals that glittered in the distance and had a magnetic attraction for us. Yet these goals were often not a product of heartfelt desire, but rather a result of the surroundings and circumstances in which we were born. The glitter surrounding what many of us have been taught to seek is often the man-made pearl of social convention, rather than the true jewel that lies in the heart of the oyster. We need to recognize this and to see that our conditioning, in terms of what we think we want, extends back into the earliest days and months of childhood and even before—we are literally taught from the womb what it is that humans are supposed to aspire to.

Beloveds, at this time in our development we are being asked by the intensifying presence of Light to look at the self-limiting concepts that surround us, especially concepts of who we are—to study them according to the dictates of our heart's yearning and to see what it is that we really believe we are meant to become. It is only by asking this question that we can truly become the individualized consciousness of God that we are each meant to be.

Consider this: the word "individual" comes from the roots "in" and "divi"—incapable of division, one whole, inseparable from itself. This word tells us that in the creation of each individual we are dealing with a manifestation of wholeness, something that is a totality within itself, unified in form and essence. Something that must be honored and maintained against the pressures and distortions of society as a whole, and of other individuals whom we exist in relation to. As we honor ourselves, we erect a sacred boundary around our wholeness which tells us: *I have a right to be*; I *have a right to become what I am.*

This right cannot be foreclosed by social forms, religious doctrines, or the tide of history, however repressive it may be. For it is an inalienable right, granted to us by the Creator, that we shall each manifest in wholeness that aspect of God-consciousness that we have been given. It is who we are in our deepest self; it is our color, our sound, and the song that our heart sings. This song has been present from time immemorial and before time as well. It is a song of gratitude for God's gift of consciousness to each being. The heart's song sings: *I AM THAT I AM - I AM Life, I AM Light, I AM one with God.*

Now, at the dawn of a new era, we are ready to participate in the disclosure of our individual destiny to ourselves. We are ready to discover our wholeness, our singularity.

In the process of self-discovery, each one of us will come to recognize the limiting forms and conditions that form a part of every functional society and that limit us as well. However, we must see clearly that it is not the social, economic, or religious restrictions that a society imposes that prevent us from becoming what we are meant to be. These create obstales in the process of human development that can be overcome. Infinitely more limiting than any of these external conditions is humankind's own inner sense of limitation about what each of us might be. Because of our disconnection, our *forgetting* of the truth of our limitlessness, we have often imagined ourselves to be victims of a particular social or economic circumstance. But this is not the truth of our being. The inner truth which all humans share is that we are defined by our consciousness—by our expectation of who we will become and what we will be, and not by any obstacle or limitations that imposes itself upon us.

Throughout the course of human history there have been individuals who lived according to this precept, who broke through the conditioning and repression of their time. They have been considered heroes and were indeed so to create a new path for themselves without any external support.

Yet the time has come for us to see *ourselves* as these heroes, and to write the page of our individual history according to a new light—the light from within. This light of our Soul-Self is directing us more and more to preserve our integrity by defining a boundary between our inner light and those conditions and circumstances that would adversely affect that light. For this light is the gift of God. It is the path of our true becoming and the life we are meant to have. To preserve this light, we must each assume responsiblity for its nourishment by the truth we live in each moment. We must learn to be ourselves.

There is no task more sacred for us at this time than the task of discovering the truth of our individuality within form, and our sameness in Spirit. In rediscovering this truth, we regain the sense of our own uniqueness and the uniqueness of all other individuals, in fact all other life-forms.

As we delve more deeply into our essential being, into our personality and particular forms of expression, we recognize the diversity of Creation. Yet precisely within this celebration and recognition of our selfhood do we begin to sense and feel the presence of that divinity that is present within all.

Dear ones, it is only by beginning to bow before the light within ourselves, by recognizing the sacred trust that we have been given as a result of inhabiting bodies, that we can begin also to bow before the light in others, who must be seen as having an equal right to be themselves. The light of the Divine shines within the righteous person and the criminal alike— within the kind and the cruel. For those beings who are misguided in the choice of their actions and who cause harm to others are equal children of God, pursuing their own path according to the challenges and opportunities that each soul has created for itself. Therefore, it is necessary to discriminate between the individual being of light and the individual action, and in doing so, to develop a way of being which preserves our own sacred boundary while acknowledging the sacred boundaries of all others.

This does not mean condoning all actions. For actions themselves can be harmful or benevolent and therefore need to be encouraged or resisted according to our sense of truth and rightness. But it does mean adopting the principle that Gandhi, Martin Luther King, Jr., Jesus, Buddha and other beings of old lived and taught—the principle and practice of *harmlessness*. Through this practice we allow all life to express itself, and do not interfere with the right of any to exist. Yet we prevent those actions from occurring which interfere with *our* right to be, and the rights of those we love and serve.

To practice harmlessness is no easy task, but it is a necessary one and one which we must each attempt at this time. For as the light without illumines the light within, we will find ourselves feeling more strongly and more enthusiastically about certain things which seem to foster our growth, and more vulnerable to the temptation of judging all those who do not meet our inner standard of how things ought to be. The danger in feeling the expansion of self from within is precisely this: that we begin to judge others who appear to be less conscious or less illuminated than ourselves. This perception can polarize the world as greatly as any other has, dividing humanity into "we" and "they." It can create a world filled with a new kind of judgment based on spiritual principle wrongly applied, and therefore limit the penetration of the Christ consciousness into our hearts. As we expand we must seek to let go of judgment as well, for only in this way does the heart open further. We must allow the sacred boundary to remain around each and every child of God, granting each one our inner permission to pursue her own path, in her own time.

Know that there is no right way to God, and there is no dead end or wrong turn. Understand that all impasses are only impasses within time, and that each eventually results in a breakthrough to a new solution in order to resolve the impasse. There is truly no point in human development, no situation, and no event that does not foster growth and change, for this is part of God's plan. Failures occur and mistakes are made, yet all beings grow in Light, and none are excluded from this appointed path. Therefore let us learn to be tolerant of those whose paths differ from ours and to recognize our spiritual family everywhere: in those whom we meet as friends, and in those whom we meet as adversaries. For all are struggling toward the same end, and all inhale the same Divine breath that breathes through us.

PAX

For we are each to become stars in the firmament, and jewels in the necklace of heaven. And that which binds us to the starry sky—to planets and galaxies and tiny seeds of corn falling from the husk—that which binds everything is the force of Spirit, holding all in Its loving consciousness...

Chapter 7

The Journey Home (Part I.)

Beloveds, the Light of consciousness sends its penetrating rays into the land of doubt and despair that the weary may become joyful and those who are tired find new strength. This Light is not to wrap itself in the clothing of former pleasures, for that time is past. Instead, it is to reveal the joy of the present moment, the knowledge that all is as it must be—the Word of God vibrating throughout the Universe—the certain knowledge of the journey home.

That which is built by human hands—pyramids, kingdoms, great works of art—will come and go, even those that appear to last forever. Yet the one truth that cannot change is the truth that the eternity of God exists within each moment and can be seen by eyes that seek the sacred.

This truth of the perfection of each moment is vaster than any other, for it brings together all truths pertaining to the unity of the Universe, the interrelation of souls, and the glory of that which is and that which is becoming. Only through timeless eyes, unconditioned by the needs of space, time, and embodiment, can this perfection be seen in its full beauty. *For there is not one stone in the Universe, not one grain of sand not connected at every moment to the sacred purpose of the Creator.* That Word that moves through the Universe continually is forever bringing into manifestation that which is needed to promote consciousness and its growth.

We need only turn within to a place of quiet and peace when difficulties confront us or when the appearance of things becomes confused. To reconnect with the heart of peace which tells us time and time again that all is well and that we have been seeing with the eyes of fear, rather than the eyes of truth.

Lofty ideas emerging from civilization's advanced state of knowledge, exquisite displays of form and color created by the hand of a true artist, the dream of cities built of gold and jewels—these are as nothing in their glory when compared to the realization of the perfection of the moment. All comfort may be taken from the thought that there is never a false step in the constantly unfolding consciousness of the Divine. There is never an event or circumstance whose gift of awareness is not totally right for the one who receives it. See now Beloveds: the gift of changing awareness produced by events that stimulate the unfoldment of our Spirit is the gift of the Divine Beloved to each of us, moving toward us now at an ever-increasing rate.

To greet all of life with the sacred trust of one who is willing to encounter each moment with full openness and with an absence of judgment—this is the greatness of each individual. To become so unafraid of truth that we simply experience what is, without judgment, and with a sense of gratitude for the unknown sequence of learning that each moment brings—this is what expands our souls.

All learning, in all areas of human endeavor, leads to this truth, whether we hear a symphony in the sounds of nature, or see loveliness in the gentle fall of autumn rain, or smile at the beauty of an infant's smile—or none of these, but rather feel an absence of love in the day's outpouring of moments and events. In the presence of the conscious-ness of beauty, and also in the presence of pain, there is growth and expansion.

For we are each to become stars in the firmament, and jewels in the necklace of heaven. And that which binds us to the starry sky—to planets and galaxies and tiny seeds of corn falling from the husk—that which binds everything is the force of Spirit, holding all in Its loving consciousness, knowing each mind and heart, each pebble and star, and dancing through each. In dancing, it brings us all into knowledge of each other.

Therefore fear not when judgments and expectations appear to cloud the vision of perfection. For the perfect *is*, whether we witness it or not. And as we strive toward real-ization we engage in a process of letting go of judgment of what "should be" more and more. When we have let go of it altogether, we will see a newly created world—one in which forms sparkle with life and dance in playful sur-render to the current animating them. One in which the Tree of Life appears to us in its full meaning and glory, and in which we meet the Divine face to face.

As children of God, it is but a step from the practice of judging to the release of judgment. Yet a step that is diffi-cult for many to take. For the fear of pain conditions and invites the experience of pain when expectations are dis-appointed and needs left unmet. If we could but see that even in death there is only the perfection of each moment of dying, and of learning from that openness—there would never again be fear in our hearts. And in the more ordinary moments of life's drama, if we could simply accept the love that is being shown to us as a child would accept a brightly colored toy placed in its little hand, then we would see an end to fear and pain.

God is within all things, and there is no time or place in which God is not. The consciousness of Light brings this truth to us more and more as we for our part, let go of those barriers that we create within ourselves to the reception of this truth. These barriers are formed of the judgments we make of ourselves and others, and of the sacred moment itself, in order to maintain a sense of the "rightness" of how *we* think life should be.

Beloveds, there is no time but *now*, in each moment, to practice releasing our hold on our *concept* of life. There is no time but *now* to experience life just as it is, without adornment by our rational and story- telling minds. Life, just plainly being itself, reflecting the grace and glory of the One Mind that holds all minds within Itself.

PAX

The single and only prerequisite on any path for contacting the Light within, is the desire to know God—*the Creator and ground of our being.*

Chapter 8

The Journey Home (Part II.)

Beloveds, open your hearts, open your minds, open the skin of your skin, the eyes of your eyes, and the ears of your ears, until the innermost core of your being yearns for the Light of Spirit. Then and only then will the angelic host descend and speak with one voice into your waiting heart and the Word of God make itself felt from the base of the spine to the top of the head. For the victory of longing over despair is the victory of that which brings the personality to the Light of the Divine through the power of the force of love.

There is no one practice that is necessary in this unfoldment other than the practice of loving devotion to the Divine and loving surrender of oneself to the Light. The practice of letting go of self can be done in many ways: through formal meditation or prayer, through service to others, and through the consecration of each action of daily life to the will of God. These are the different paths to the One, and there shall always remain several, for each being chooses according to his or her soul's light.

The single and only prerequisite on any path for contacting the Light within is the desire to know God—the Creator and ground of our being.

Let this truth be understood: the path to God is strewn with the flowers of devotion, tossed at the sacred feet of He Who Waits Beyond the Light, as well as with thorns that are the product of imperfect love—love that seeks its own satisfaction still, rather than the satisfaction of God. These thorns are the wounds the ego feels while it still resists giving up its own authority as it travels into Light. And whether a person will experience more thorns or flowers at a point along the way is difficult to say, for this is not a matter of one lifetime only, but of a path traversed in many lifetimes, the challenge being met little by little.

Beloveds, the goal of every path is wholeness—the reunion of self with Self, the Divine Beloved. To reach this goal we must desire this reunion with the pulse of each heartbeat and with the breath of each breath. The scientist may feel drawn onward by the love of Truth; the artist by the love of Beauty; and the devotee by the love of the Creator. Those who serve mankind may feel drawn by their love for humanity as a whole. There are countless forms that Love takes as it becomes Divine, and each one acts to transform us from a pattern of self-seeking and self-gratification, to a pattern of selflessness and love.

As we evolve, our longing for the Divine naturally increases. For we have been breathed through with a sacred purpose that draws us like a magnet to our destiny in consciousness, and no person and no event can change this plan for us. There are those who would quicken their movement down the Path of Light, and for them the difficulties increase and the obstacles seem larger. For instead of waiting to become the size of Goliath before taking on the challenges that must be faced, these courageous ones determine to approach all obstacles with the strength of David, much smaller but stronger in mind, in character, and in strength of purpose.

These three qualities—a clear mind, a strong character, and a dedicated purpose, are needed by those who choose to overcome the obstacles presented by the ego—by those who choose victory *now*. Yet even with these three traits, the force that above all others *destroys* the inner barriers and makes defeat for the ego inevitable, is the growing love of Spirit which permeates every atom of our being and which is increasingly felt by the conscious self.

We need to anticipate that this love will not grow without difficulty and that the ego will grumble at the price it pays for what is being given up. For the ego's development from the beginning has been based on the principle of self-seeking and the fulfillment of personal desire, and it sees itself now losing the possiblity for fulfillment instead of gaining it. Understand that through countless lifetimes, as we sought to learn and grow as souls, the ego was necessary to help us maneuver on the physical plane once trust in the Divine source of guidance was gone. Therefore now, at the point of reconnecting with this Source, we must treat the ego with compassion and understanding. For it has served its purpose well and brought us to a point in evolution where we can begin to surrender the lesser consciousness of our individuality to that which is greater than ourselves of which we are a part. In this process of surrender we do love our individuality. What we lose is our *attachment* to the fulfillment of desire, our self- importance, and the need to manage and control our life.

This relinquishing of control by the ego occurs in slow stages for many and at a more rapid rate for some. It is a most sacred transition in spiritual awareness, and one which produces what has been called "the dark night of the soul." For in this process the ego experiences its own dying, while the soul separates itself from the ego, the personality, and the desire-nature. In this manner the soul begins to journey forth to God, in order to unite itself to That which it loves and perceives itself to have lost.

It is said that it is in darkness that the soul must journey and in the absence of gratification. For if it saw before it a clear point to which it must go or clear guidance or reward of any kind, even a spiritual kind, the soul would again reattach itself to the need to feel gratified, the need to feel reassured, or the need to feel secure. Thus, without any of these conditions, the soul journeys forth in darkness, without guidance, led forward only by the persistence of its faith that it will find what it seeks at the outcome of the journey.

Beloveds, all help is given to those who travel in darkness, though they may at times not perceive it to be so. For God does not allow those who seek Him to seek in vain, and each one who abandons self in order to find the true Source of being will at all times be supported in that seeking. The sign that God is with each one is the increasing intensity of the desire to seek the Light, for that desire could not be created by the ego or the personal self, since the soul abandons and dismisses all qualities of the ego, which now appear to hold it back from continuing on its way. Therefore the seeking itself must, for a time, serve as the sign that each of us is being led along the precise path of surrender that we must take, in order to most quickly find our way Home.

The ego will become distressed, and will create inner obstacles to convince the personality that the choice is wrong to seek the Light. And truly, from the ego's standpoint the choice *is* wrong. For the surrender of control over our lives as a measure of trust in Divine guidance is precisely what the ego has been created to supplant.

It is as if an understudy has been given a part to play for an actor that is ill and temporarily absent. When the actor comes back restored to good health, the understudy no longer remembers that he has only been filling in, and wants to remain in the part he has been assigned to play. In like manner the ego has been assigned a part to play on the stage of history, a part which grew out of the need for an overseer on the physical plane. This overseer was to temporarily act in lieu of Divine guidance which, it was felt, could no longer effectively manage or direct the human drama. But the undertudy stayed, and the history of the human drama then became the history of the growth of the ego. On the positive side this created effective personalities, and fostered the process of differentiation among individuals. On the negative side, increasing fear based on separation began to spread, and the need for power and control over one another began to develop.

The stage of history is now set for the ego to release its hold on the part it has been playing and for humankind to once again realize the presence of the Divine director. What is necessary at this time, even more than *belief* in this truth, is just a little willingness to let go, bit by bit, of thoughts of what "I want" and what "I must have." To experiment in small areas of our lives with turning decision-making over to Divine will can produce a spaciousness in our everyday thought process that relieves the mind as well as the body of accumulated stress. This also convinces the conscious self, little by little, of the safety in surrender. For the mind and the body both feel the pressure of having to calculate and figure out how to manage, moment by moment, with the pressures of life pressing up against us day by day and year by year. Releasing just a little bit of our everyday decision-making to Divine will means being willing to say: "Here, I don't know what is best. You decide this for me." And Beloveds, it is this invitation to Spirit to resume its place in our lives which actually strengthens and intensifies the speed of forward movement into the Light of God-consciousness.

Compassion at all times for the ego and its wants must remain. Otherwise self-blame for continuing to have desires will appear along with all the other self-criticisms that the ego maintains. Yet in time, the little willingness to "not know," and to trust that the truth of our inner self will be revealed, will lead to the Spirit of Truth and Light manifesting in our lives in ways that we would not have considered possible.

Over and over again as the words of fear and denial come to us, to remind us that we are foolish to trust in Divine inspiration, we must remember the faith of Noah, who embarked on the ocean without knowing when land would be sighted, or of David, who knew not how he could vanquish the giant Goliath, or of the prophets of old who held the vision for others—that God *would* lead the people out of the house of bondage. As we remember these ancient ones who are part of our history, let us know that we too are being called to leave the house of our individual bondage—that bondage which the ego exacts from us that causes us to see a world of fear and mistrust, rather than a world of love and hope. That bondage which causes us to live with a sense of rivalry in relation to others, and a need to defend who we are and what we have from them. That bondage takes from us trust and hope—the solace of our souls—and leaves us feeling lost within an inner landscape of doubt, despair, and confusion.

These, Beloveds, are the victories of the ego manifesting throughout history: the creation of war and of the fear of our enemies; the creation of kingdoms and dynasties—both corporate and political—which serve the few at the expense of the many; the creation of cities which abandon the principle of living in harmony with nature; the development of egocentrism—applied both to individual self-interest and to collective self-interest when we consider ourselves to be more important than other races or than other life-forms. The ego has also been responsible for the greatness of our achievement in many areas of knowledge and thought, in the study of nature and society and of man himself. However these achievements have not been balanced by attention to the voice of the soul, which struggled to be heard throughout history as life, civilized life, became more and more out of balance.

There is a Universe of life to discover, Beloveds, of intelligences that are different from ours—both lower and higher in the hierarchy of consciousness. We, humankind, are pivotal in the Earth's plan for its own expanding awareness, and in the Divine plan for the solar system. But we are not *more* important than Life itself—the life pervading all equally.

As we reassign the ego to its rightful place as manager of a certain portion of our transactions on the physcial plane, we once again move into balance and harmony with all forms of life. We once again feel our affinity with plants and animals and with the Spirit that gives them life, with stars and galaxies and the life that moves within them as well. This then is the gift to come, the gift of universal knowing: *one life, one breath, one Spirit.*

Beloveds, this gift is being revealed to us bit by bit even now, for the time of revelation has come. Soon humankind shall share in the joy of knowing itself to be forever protected and forever loved. Therefore rest easy, for the dawn of a New Age is here, and signals of its presence are flashing through our consciousness, awakening us to the glory of true being.

PAX

There is no mystery more profound than this: how God draws us into the web of love, that we may share Her joy and Her radiance. There is no mystery more worthy of understanding than the mystery of that love that binds the Universe. For the very atoms of our bodies are bound together by the force of Love, as are the stars within the heavens, and the galaxies themselves.

Chapter 9

The Divine Plan

Beloveds, the mystery of creation remains forever concealed in the mind of the Creator, yet has been received, in part by minds that have transcended the limitations of space and time, soaring to the heights of God-realization. Such are the sages of old who have handed down to humanity the patterns of thought that form the basis for the great world religions.

The teaching that there is a divinely ordained plan for human development in place at each and every moment is an idea whose importance for us grows each day. Hindu saints and sages considering this plan have called it the "in-breathing" and "out-breathing" of God. Through contemplation they have "seen" that God having breathed the Universe into creation and directed Spirit to penetrate matter more and more, at some point begins to draw the Universe back toward Himself.

Beloveds, we are now at that turning point from out-breath to in-breath. We, as a people have descended as fully as possible into engagement with the material world and its values. In the time just ahead we will be guided to reverse our attention and direction, to return it once again toward the Divine Creator Who seeks an alignment in consciousness with each of us.

There is no action that must be taken in order to prepare for this shift. What is needed is an attunement of mind and heart to "prepare the way of the Lord." Just as John the Baptist prepared the way for the arrival of Jesus, so too are we each being asked to prepare the way for the advent of the revelation of the Christ.

The turning point has this effect as well: that those who resist the attraction of the Divine call will feel their hearts harden to the spiritual qualities that will be felt by many. In this way, the world may become divided into those who respond to the turning point by allowing the change to take place within, and those who flee in fear from this awakening. The choice belongs to each of us within time. Beyond time we are all one with the plan.

And the plan for humanity is unequivocal: that all beings shall come to know their Creator, and that the Creator shall know all of material plane existence through the consciousness of His children. For God wishes to see the world through our eyes, and to hear the sound of the birds through our ears. We are now and have always been an extension of the consciousness of God within the physical world. And just as an official will send a scouting party ahead into new terrain, so too has God asked us to see and hear and know the life of the physical plane, in order to unite His consciousness with the form of its embodiment.

It is our Divine purpose then, to penetrate the world of matter with the consciousness of Spirit—to live this within our physical bodies, and to see the light of Spirit in all that surrounds us.

No writing will convince us of this truth. It must be understood with the heart.

The experience of revelation for countless generations supports this same vision: that God's purpose for mankind is that all shall know Him. This is the meaning of the advent of the Christ consciousness.

It is because God's nature is Love that this is true. For it is in the nature of Love to extend its boundaries and to seek to love more, once it feels the impulse at all. Those who have been in love will remember that it is a state of great exaltation—a state of feeling that the beloved is beautiful and priceless, and that all that surrounds oneself is blessed with an aura of benevolence. And as one in love blesses all that she sees with her radiance, so too does the response of joy return to that one from those whom she meets.

We are in that relationship to the Creator. *We* are the beloved of the Most High, and the object of that Love at all times. As we feel this Love, we have the capacity to reflect it back to the Beloved from whom it comes. In the process of this spiritual reflection we experience ourselves as the beloved of God, the lover of God, and the expanding lovingness itself.

There is no mystery more profound than this: how God draws us into the web of love, that we may share Her joy and Her radiance. There is no mystery more worthy of understanding than the mystery of that love that binds the Universe. For the very atoms of our bodies are bound together by the force of Love as are the stars within the heavens and the galaxies themselves. There is no limit to the infinite supply of Love flowing from the heart of God— singing of the oneness of all that is, beckoning all who hear to chant the song of unity and of being.

Love that creates worlds and Universes as if they were children cannot be undertood in human terms. For this Love spins itself out in endless creation, rejoicing in the birth and growth of each new being as we rejoice in the creation of our own children. Rejoicing in the existence of each form as a reflection of Itself. As if God, through form, sees Himself in some way for the first time clearly.

We speak in metaphor using human analogy because we do not yet have the language to imagine the nature of Love that is so far beyond the human. That I AM THAT I AM chooses to become human and to become all else in the manifested Universe cannot be fathomed except by human analogy. And this way of understanding by analogy is correct: for the principle of consciousness teaches us that we are all mirrors for each other, as we are all teachers for each other. In relation to the worlds of Spirit and Matter, the same truth holds—*As Above, So Below*—mirrors of Spirit and Matter. This *principle of correspondence* teaches us that in order to understand the Most High, we may rightfully look at the physical world as a mirror of the higher meaning. Therefore, let us imagine that as we look at ourselves to understand God, so too does God look at us to see Himself more clearly.

As Above, So Below—the principle of correspondence resounds through the Universe, telling of the endless stream of life which has no beginning and no end, but which circles back into itself—the Alpha and Omega of creation.

Alpha and Omega: all peoples, all spiritual traditions, hold this in some form as the image of the Divine—that the Universe is a circle, complete unto Itself. And that what appears to have a beginning and an end only seems to do so within the framework of time and space. In reality, there is only ongoingness. For the circle is unbroken and our perceptions of linear time are misconceptions based on the limitations of the concrete mind. Limitations based on the idea of separateness. In reality we have never left the wholeness of the circle; we are at all times joined with the oneness of all that is.

It is the return to this consciousness of the whole that marks the turning point that lies just ahead in human history. It is the recognition of the relationship between Alpha and Omega—between the Creative Source and the indwelling Spirit within matter.

This turning point will bring humanity's consciousness further along the circle of growth to an awareness of the passage Home. And we as children of the Earth and Sky, as children of Alpha and Omega, are to know our greatness as part of the circle of life. We are to experience our presence among the stars as brothers and sisters in Light. We are to know the Life that moves within the atom and within ourselves—the Divine life penetrating all. For we are part of the Earth's plan for rejoining the Universal Light and part of the Creator's plan for all beings.

I AM THAT I AM—the knowlege of Thyself as Light and Love shall be.

PAX

PART II: *Truth*

We are the form that Spirit has created to witness the mystery of life within form, and the marriage of Matter and Spirit. We are the awareness of Spirit seeking the Beloved within the material plane. And all that we are, and all that we see, teaches us daily that what we choose to do *in life cannot bring to us the sense of peace and harmony and that deeper sense of knowing, that is arrived at only through the experience of being.*

Chapter 10

The Mystery of Being

When the leaves fall from the trees or the snow sparkles in bright winter sun, the human heart is stirred to ask about the origin of such beauty as it opens wider to the sense of transcendent order within the natural world. At these times, our senses declare their joy to us at being present at a moment of perception when what is, is all that needs to be. At these times, the leaves speak to us of the presence of God as they fall; the sun shimmers with the radiance of spiritual blessing, and the air itself tells us of unknown truths—of the energy moving through all of space. And who are we humans, we wonder, that we have been given this perception of mystery, yet still feel separated within our own skins from the rest of life?

Beloveds, we are the form that Spirit has created, to witness the mystery of life within form, and the marriage of Matter and Spirit. We are the awareness of Spirit seeking the Beloved within the material plane. And all that we are and all that we see, teaches us daily that what we choose to do in life cannot bring to us the sense of peace and harmony, and that deeper sense of knowing that is arrived at only through the experience of being.

Many children of God do not yet understand the difference between *being* and *doing*. They feel they do not know how to "just be." And in truth, though this is the simplest thing once one knows how to do it, the mind does not easily allow this kind of relaxing to take place without protesting that "there is more work to do." There *is* more work to do Beloveds, and it is the work of learning to *be* in the present moment.

For we have not come to this Earth plane in order to become successful in the stock market, or to build muscles in a gymnasium, or to win a beauty contest. We have come here to recognize our connection with life around us and to express the life within us. These two streams, the outer and the inner, move through our lives at all times; at each moment, they present us with the ground of our being.

On the outer level, we might see a scene before us on a day outdoors. It may be a scene of beauty at a lake or meadow, or perhaps the trees in a neighbor's backyard. Whatever we see before us is part of the dance of life *at that moment of time* in which we perceive it. And we are meant to take part in this dance by acknowledging our fullest response to our perceptions.

How many people do we know that go to a park with a picnic basket with friends or family and spend the time talking and cooking, rather than walking around to smell and feel the air, to feel the Earth's softness beneath their feet, and to watch the pattern of sunlight as it filters through tall trees? This is an example of the need *to do* expressed in a very ordinary situation. We select *part* of an experience to pay attention to such as the need to cook, or to set the table, or to acknowledge friends, while treating the rest of the experience indifferently.

Being involves us in responding totally to the experience we are in, the setting of the moment as well as the persons within it. In order to do this, we must stop the internal dialogue which tells us: "This is what you should do now, and now, and now... " The voice which speaks in this way has been handed down to us through countless generations of social convention.

To be in the moment is to dance with life as it presents itself—to embrace it fully through our response to it. This is really what it means to understand the sacredness of life and the presence of God within it.

Beingness is not something that we have to learn. Rather, we have to un-learn those attitudes which interfere with our right to be.

For example, we stand in line at a check-out counter of a supermarket and the person in front of us reminds us of someone in our family that we haven't seen in years— perhaps a grandparent that has died. We stare and stare at the physical likeness. Social convention dictates that we do not speak of this "coincidence," in order to spare possible embarrassment to the other person as well as to ourselves. Yet the joy of the moment in seeing a beloved grandparent reappear wants to express itself as it stirs up love within us. Often, the inner and the outer streams of life have an energy and a momentum that seems to connect them. In being faithful to the meaning of this moment, what would be natural might be to effusively greet (if not hug) that person who reminds us of our grandparent. Or, though this seems quite ridiculous to the rational mind, to offer them some gesture or service out of the love that has arisen within us. Yet how many of us act out of the impulse of the moment that arises so strongly within our hearts? How many would express the heartfelt gladness of meeting to this stranger, who is not really a stranger, and allow whatever developed to develop? Perhaps that person would be shy, and would respond matter-of-factly to our gesture of friendship. Perhaps she would be touched to be beheld with such loving warmth. Can we release the judgment about this and act out of the fullness of our heart's responding?

All of life presents us with similar encounters—times in

which the heart directs us to an expression that is completely natural to the moment, but that is deemed "inappropriate" according to certain codes of behavior. Even at a picnic in the country we are being invited to encounter the trees and the little woodland flowers that grow beneath them. And yet how difficult it is to take the time to notice them, and to develop a relationship with them.

Beloveds, we are coming closer to a time when we each will have to choose between the dictates of the heart's knowing and the logical rules set down by social conscience and convention. For our world is in the midst of great change—socially, politically, spiritually, and we have many choices to make about which part of the world we wish to align ourselves with. The choice to *be*—to express the life-force that arises within us can shape the entire course of our lives if we allow it, influencing not only our decisions about where we live and with whom, but also our daily activities and the rhythms we create for ourselves within our work lives.

In a state of attunement to our being, we are enabled to drop the distinction between work-time and "free-time." We become free to be ourselves all of the time, even if we function within the structure of a society or an organization that requires us to act in specific ways. The state of freedom is an inner state, created by the awareness that at each moment we are choosing how to respond to life, given an awareness of all the circumstances. In this state we need not fear that we will embarrass ourselves by acting inappropriately, for when we are truly sensing the energies moving within the inner and the outer life-streams, we cannot help but honor all aspects of our being and express not only the best possible response, but also one that feels most right to us.

Dear ones, we each have much more "free time" than we have given ourselves—time in which to express the life within us. We have countless opportunities to open to the spontaneity, playfulness, and lovingness that is naturally ours, when we allow it to be.

The dance of life goes on and on, and like the Pied Piper of Hamelin it leads us forward in step with a tune that captivates us and sets our feet to dancing. In this dance, we become partners with the life force itself which seeks expression through us. This greatest of all gifts, freely given by Spirit, asks us to take the inner impulse that rises up within us and give it form—not just artistic form, though this is a possiblity for many of us. But expressive form in which we joyously share our perception of life with other beings, that they too may respond joyfully to life within their own form of expression.

When we lie on our backs staring at the stars on a summer night, we wonder at the nature of that greater Being that has set the stars and planets in their course within the firmament of heaven. We wonder about the importance of humanity in relation to that immense sky. Beloveds, we cannot help but wonder, for wonder is part of the natural response of being and of human observation to what surrounds us. Wonder and its twin-sister delight have been entrusted to us as a legacy of Spirit, that we may respond to God's presence from the place of God within our hearts.

Therefore, if we were each to resolve to allow ourselves to experience wonder at what we see around us all of the time, we would not be far from viewing human life the way the angels do: we would sense the mysterious connection of love and joy that brings us close to the stranger in a check-out line; we would tresure the delicacy of the tiniest of flowers beneath a giant hemlock; we would wonder at our own silliness that pushes its way up from a place deep within us and that asks us in the midst of seriousness to become attuned to the child within.

Our being speaks to us of the need to open to each moment with trust and with wonder, and to give it our fullest attention. To trust that *each* moment is as filled with Divine presence and meaning as any other, and to let go of inner judgments we still carry that set priorities on what we think we should be experiencing.

Open therefore to the sun dear ones, and to the moon and stars, and to each other, and to the sounds of animals, and the feel of rain, and the colors of clothing, and the wrinkles around the eyes of a friend, and the feeling of expansion within your hearts. In ruling nothing out of our willingness to experience, we become fully alive, fully human, and fully Divine.

PAX

Waiting, while attuning to Divine purpose, is often an entry point into living in a state of Grace... What is being created often in the waiting time is the consciousness that all good things come from God.

Chapter 11

The Beginning of Healing

It is an old truth for many of us that what we send out into the Universe shall return to us in kind, for the great law of Life, the Law of Karma is a law of justice and of order, governing the sequence of human events. What is less easily recognized is that this same law is the engine which propels the entire Universe forward into greater wholeness. The Law of Karma applies to stars as well as people, to insects as well as galaxies. In the case of the insect, it is a law which applies to the species, rather than to the individual entity, for groups that do not experience free choice as humans do have group karma. This applies to all kingdoms in which individual consciousness has not yet evolved.

All beings who possess free will, however, are subject to the law of individual karma, which balances all actions in the Universe in such a way as to turn everything to the highest good. The most negative action that we can think of on the human plane—for example that of deliberately harming a child, will have repercussions for the individual performing that action sooner or later. That individual will feel and know the result of his behavior one day, perhaps in a later life through conscious identification as a receiver of abuse. However it happens, at some point the soul will readjust the inner values which allowed that personality to perform the harmful act.

All karma has as its goal the outcome of expanding consciousness, by bringing into balance those impulses and actions that do not follow the highest principles of Truth and Love. There is no exception to this rule, for it forms the basis for the evolution of the Universe at one level, and for all beings within it.

Karma and consciousness are inextricable in their meaning and effects and there is no occasion when an event which *seems* to occur accidentally actually does so. Karma is part of the creative Life force moving through matter— literally affecting the response of people to us, our body's response, and the patterning of life-events as well. The events which come into our lives are physically manifested energy patterns produced by the Law of Karma that bring into our consciousness alterations in those attitudes that are in need of healing. There is no event or circumstance within human experience that is not influenced by the Law of Karma, until we reach the point in evolution where all of our actions are attuned to Divine will, and all choices serve the purposes of the Creator. At that point, karma no longer serves its purpose as the engine governing human progress; instead, it is superceded by Divine Grace, which moves increasingly through the life of the individual.

The healing potential of karma has been misunderstood in popular consciousness, where individuals still do not see themselve as responsible for the creation of their own lives. When we are willing to blame life for being unfair to us and to blame God for not having our best interets at heart, it will seem to us that the world is a disorderly series of accidents happening to us according to our luck. This view is the opposite of what actually is true. There is nothing that is more orderly than the procession of challenges and opportunities within individual history, which guarantee to each soul a chance to redeem its consciousness from all aspects of negativity that that soul has accumulated, and to bring consciousness each day more fully into the light of Truth.

What has been referred to as "negative" karma—namely, events that are experienced as personally painful—expands consciousness by requiring that individual to shift perspectives in the area of values—to look at what he or she has previously considered to be important from a new point of view. *All* pain serves this purpose and all karma serves this purpose. What has been considered to be positive karma—the "lucky star" that weaves its way through the destiny of certain individuals is more than the reward for past efforts in the direction of goodness and truth. It is that, but it is also the furthering of that individual's consciousness into harmonious alignment with the cosmos, through the experience of *gratitude*. If we were to have rewards and blessings heaped on upon us throughout life and were not thankful to God, we would witness new negative karma being generated by attitudes of pride and selfishness that would begin to color our lifestyle and choices. The object of a blessed life is not this, but rather greater experience of attunement and alignment with the Universal flow. If we were to take a blessed life, an abundant life, and store up riches for the self while not giving to others, the karma generated would sooner or later alter the outpicturing on the material plane of what would no longer be considered inner wealth.

So, dear ones, let us become aware of karma as a steadily operating condition, influenced both by the thoughts and actions that operate within our awareness and by those that operate below the threshold of consciousness as well. When these thoughts and actions are directed to the purpose of living according to the highest principles that we can conceive of—how God would have us live—then as we follow our path we live increasingly in the light of Grace, and past karma is progressively reduced.

It is primarily the motivating thought patterns that are healed by the balancing action of karma, for these are behind whatever behavior the human being manifests on the physical plane. If we seek to express only love, only truth, then the life that we will eventually bring into reality will be a life filled with love, truth, and harmony with our surroundings.

We often hear complaints from loved ones who are trying to lead good and worthy lives, that despite their best efforts, despite the fact that they have lived unselfishly and with care to God's commandments, bad things continue to happen. The position of Job in the Bible is an illustration of this, but not only Job. There are men and women in the Bible—Sarah, Abraham's wife; Elizabeth, the mother of John the Baptist; David, the shepherd-King and author of the *Psalms*—who had to wait some time for their wishes to be fulfilled or their destiny to manifest itself. *Waiting, while attuning to Divine purpose, is often an entry point into living in a state of Grace.*

For in these biblical instances of waiting, as well as in our own, what is often being acquired is a deepening of the capacity to accept Divine will with love and trust, and to surrender personal will. *What is being created often in the waiting time is the consciousness that all good things come from God.*

It is hard for us to appreciate this sometimes when we wish to have our "just rewards" materialize faster, in keeping with what we hold to be our "good behavior." We need to remember three things, particularly at times of waiting: first, that we are transforming those aspects of our consciousness that need healing (from this life and from other lifetimes). Second, that we cannot judge or know why we are not more immediately blessed with an answer to our prayers or the fulfillment of our desire, and that this *un-knowing* is a necessary part of our healing experience. And third, that what we consider to be best for ourselves, what we consider to be what we most truly want, may or may not be the truth of our heart's desire.

What *is* true is that spiritual intelligence, the intelligence of our Higher Self, can see far more clearly into our hearts and minds in terms of what our soul is seeking, than can the conscious part of us which is but a small part of what is really our intelligence. We need to assume, as we go through a period of waiting for what we wish to appear, that the Universe is responding to us in terms of what we really *need* to have happen, for the purposes of our soul's growth in awareness, rather than what we *want* to have happen, from the standpoint of our conscious minds. Therefore, in the process of waiting and of attuning to Divine will, it is useful to keep this prayer in our hearts:

"Lord, may I receive what I need from Thee."

This thought and prayer create a sense of patience within us, and lead to a growing awareness of that deeper level of asking that is always beyond the obvious. For the nature of Truth is that it is layered within our consciousness, and as we are willing to go beyond the topmost level of our thinking—ie. "what is true is that which I think is true"—the next layer of Truth begins to reveal itself to our mind which is now open.

Therefore, when we wait, let us wait in hope. For hope is the mother of all things. And when we cry, let us cry out to God to teach us the nature of Truth within us, that we may know ourselves at the deepest level of essential being, and come to understand our power as the creators of our lives.

We have focused on karma as a healing and balancing force within individual consciousness. Over time, the Law of Karma heals in another way as well. This is through the help it offers in teaching us how we create our lives *through thought*. Through the effect of karma, our consciousness begins to understand the relationship between cause and effect, slowly and unconsciously, and each of us begins to purify our thoughts as well as our actions. An unconscious perception emerges over aeons of time that certain patterns of thought and feeling are not constructive for our own lives or the lives of others. And thus in the *historical* context, the willingness to accept new ideas and new values is born.

Understanding the power of thought to create reality is a major step forward in the soul's evolution on the planes of matter. It is an inner knowing of the truth, however vague, that each thought liberates energy into the Universe.

In fact, the mind is a powerful tool given to each Spirit, so that it may learn of its oneness with God. Let us remember that God has created the entire Universe through the power of thought, and that in like manner, as we recall our heritage as children of God, what we conceive of within our lives shall ultimately be. The biblical teaching:

"Seek, and ye shall find; knock, and it shall be opened; Ask and ye shall receive."

has several meanings. It tells us both of the nature of a loving God who wishes to respond to the needs of Her children, *and*, on an esoteric level, of the principle of thought creating form.

"Ask, and ye shall receive."

Dear ones, if we only knew how true this was we would never allow ourselves for a second to harbor within our minds a thought that was not worthy of us, whether in relation to ourselves or to others. For when we think depressing, fearful, or angry thoughts, we create an expectation in our conscious minds that the circumstances which have produced these thoughts will continue, or if not yet present that they will appear.

All expectations, whether positive or negative, are thoughts which have a powerful effect on the reality that emerges. Even if we have a fear, say, of being laughed at, and say consciously: "Oh, may I never be laughed at. Today I hope that nobody laughs at me." Though we are wishing away a painful circumstance consciously, the energy of that thought is actually bringing into our surroundings events that can be interpreted in the light: "Yes, perhaps right here someone is laughing at me."

We need therefore, through our understanding of the Law of Karma, through our belief in the healing power of the material Universe to bring us into greater consciousness, and through our understanding of the power of thought, to become each day more responsible citizens of this planet. Each one of us is being healed and made whole during our journey on planet Earth, just through the accumulation of multiple life experiences. We are each day moving forward in learning and in Light, and life itself is our greatest teacher. We need to become more aware of the ways in which we are contributing to or detracting from the healing of the planet and of other beings upon it, by the thoughts we think about them.

Let us therefore eliminate from our minds all but thoughts of love for life on Earth, all but acceptance of Spirit's graciousness manifesting behind all forms. Let us know that as we walk in the thought of this graciousness and goodness, even in the midst of difficulty, we will be bringing our awareness to the state of Grace that is always potentially present. In this way, we will find the gate to the Kingdom of Heaven upon Earth, which stands just in front of us.

PAX

When the heart is a tranquil lake, in which only the ripples of Divine Will find their expression, then that lake is able to reflect clearly both the truth about oneself and the truth about the world.

Chapter 12

The Path of Purification

Part I. The Sceptre of Purity and the Sword of Discrimination

Beloveds, to become pure is to wield power over all those clamoring impulses within us that would set their own satisfaction above the love of God. It is to develop the power of Spirit to such a degree that rule is established over all motives, all thoughts, and all words that we speak that do not reflect the truth of our Divine nature. Purity is like an honored guest that we invite into our hearts to counsel and advise us, so that we may have the strength and clarity to eliminate from consciousness all residues of thought built on the misconception of our separation from the Divine.

The power of a pure heart lies in its invulnerability to evil. The pure can walk through a crowd or through the darkest of nights alone without harm befalling them. Cloaked in love of Spirit, they are untouched by negative influences that surround them, for there is nothing within themselves for these negative energies to hold onto. And so anger, fear, envy—the negative emotions of the astral plane that are so common in daily life—find no place to cling in beings that are pure.

Dear ones, the night may be dark around us, yet clothed in purity we are filled with Light; we ride the purest of white horses to the goal we have set, and the rays of light that we emit defend us against all who would stop us on our way.

With the sceptre of purity comes the sword of discrimination. This sword is the reward for those who have pursued the Holy Grail successfully. It brings with it the ability to see truth uncluttered by the eyes of personal desire, truth unclouded by the fogs of social perception, and truth undisturbed by the longings in one's heart.

When the heart is a tranquil lake, where only the ripples of Divine will find their expression, then that lake is able to reflect clearly both the truth about oneself and the truth about the world.

As purity is acquired the heart sees clearly how the spoken word can reflect degrees of falseness and degrees of truth, and it becoms impossible for one seeking purity to allow any word that is false to escape from her lips.

The sword of discrimination applies also to that intuitive sense which tells us of the truth within others. Without calculation or rational processes of understanding, it teaches us to recognize the real motive in the hearts of others, behind their actions and behind their words.

The sword of discrimination is the sword of Parsifal and of King Arthur. It is that primary instrument bequeathed to us as a gift of Spirit which allows us to know the intention of the Creator and to feel His goodness as it manifests throughout life. For it gives to us a sense of the "rightness" of a situation in terms of its manifesting the highest principles of Light. Holding this sword, we learn to follow the highest Truth, because we are able to sense which Truth that life presents carries more of the light of Spirit.

Those who seek purity will find a path to God uncluttered by the need to follow the dictates of a formal teaching or school of thought. For purity is its own teacher, leading us directly to the God within. It removes from us the necessity of following outer gurus, and of seeking words of truth other than those which come from the outflowing of our own hearts. Purity leads us to the inner Guru—the voice of the Divine Beloved. And as this voice is heard, it fills us with a powerful resonance that can be found again and again—in the song of being in the hearts of others, in the beauty of the sky, and in the voice of revelation which whispers to us through countless daily events of the eternal presence of Spirit in our lives.

PAX

For all losses are challenges that have concealed gifts within them—gifts of awareness and awakening.

Chapter 13

The Path of Purification

Part II: The Process of Purification

Beloveds, the path of purification involves above all, a surrender of the heart to the purposes of Spirit, that we may rise more quickly into Light. To this end, we sacrifice those pleasures of the ego which in former times were accepted as rightfully ours: the right to feel angry and to seek revenge when wronged; the right to feel envious and to take what is someone else's; the right to seek self-satisfaction at the expense of another; the right to wish another harm based on any of the motives just named.

Within the light of Spirit, we ask that these rights be replaced by the one right that transcends them all—the right to know ourselves as Divine and to inherit the Kingdom that is rightfully ours.

In purifying ourselves, what we are really doing is detaching from the wants of the ego and identifying with the motives of our higher Selves. In this process, the ego is bound to be heard protesting and complaining that what is happening to it is not fair. And this is the truth. Purification is *not* fair to the ego, for the effect of purification is to reduce the function of the ego to a far less important position that it has been accustomed to. And to eliminate altogether those desires and impulses which are the product of the consciousness of separation from God, and not the result of Divine Will expressing within us.

If our Souls are to become mirrors for the reflection of Spirit, and if we would hear the voice of our Soul, then we must learn to quiet the voices which compete with this one. These are the voices of the desire-body (the astral-mental vehicle), which repeat for us what we have been taught to want and expect from life. When at a certain point in our development, we have the support of the energy of our Soul, we begin to give less weight to the ego's voice—the voice of desire; we begin to treat it as a guest in our inner house, welcomed if it behaves properly, and unwelcome if it does not follow the rules we have set for it. The ego, accustomed to thinking of *itself* as master in our house, and to believing that *it* makes the rules, is often intolerant of this change in our attitude. Therefore it does all in its power to criticize our new way of thought in order to reestablish the former equilibrium and to maintain its authority. Eventually, as we continue to tread the path of purification and persist in following the principles of Spirit, a new balance is attained within us, one in which the ego has a voice but does not rule.

Beloveds, on the path of purification one law stands out above all others, and as we progress this law beings to influence our thoughts and actions more and more. In Hinduism it is called the law of "ahimsa" or harmlessness. In the Christian tradition it is: "do unto others as you would have others do unto you." In Judaism it is contained in the second commandment: "Love thy neighbor as thyself." This law prohibits us from taking any action, including the action of thinking, that might harm another being. As we experience this law within our purified consciousness, we see that it applies both to humans and to our relationship with all forms of life. We begin to feel within our purified awareness that all life-forms are broth-

94

ers and sisters, and whether they be large or small they are
children of God. And so we bow to the Divine essence
within each, whether the form has importance according
to man's estimation or not.

As purification begins, we begin to release judgment of
ourselves and others, and learn to recognize motives
within ourselves which, however subtlely, lead to actions
that "pay someone back" for their injury to us. For example, a person in our family says unkind words to us and
hurts our feelings. Later, they ask for a favor or make a request of us and we pretend not to hear them; or we do
hear them and then say "no." Our response is motivated
by our earlier anger or hurt and this response becomes
fully conscious in the purified mind; as it does so, we find
ourself choosing not to honor this motive.

Purification is a subtle process, for we are dealing
primarily with an understanding of *motives* and not of behaviors that might be noticed by others. As we observe
ourselves, we begin to *know* when we have *intended* to pay
someone back in kind, one hurt for another, and we find
this type of retaliation no longer acceptable.

Another example—we lose a job or do not receive a
promotion that we were expecting, or someone else gets
chosen for a position that we were striving for. After this,
we find ourselves becoming irritable and depressed. We
are sullen with our family and indifferent to comforting.
To an outsider, all of this seems understandable given the
circumstances, even reasonable. We lose a job; we feel
badly. So speaks the voice of the world. And yet as we
purify, we hear in our irritability a voice of protest against
God. We hear ourselves inwardly complaining at the injustice of a Universe that has let us down in this way. We
are assuming, with the ego, that *we* know how things are
supposed to be.

As we hear this voice of complaint from within, we begin to see how it goes against everything we have learned

about karma and about the evolution of the soul. And as we review our feelings we come again and again to the basic choice that we have to make on the path of purification, the choice between two masters—the voice of the world, and the voice of Spirit. Jesus said: *"Ye cannot serve two masters"* and this is true. We will face this choice again and again, sometimes with clarity and sometimes with a sense of failure. For the call to belief that life events are "unfortunate" or "bad luck" is the basis for the world's viewpoint, and the fundamental assumption which the ego *was created to deal with.*

If the world is chaotic as well as "unfortunate," then there had better be a force within us that is strong, resilient, correct, and in-charge, that can handle things that come up and define them for us at all times. This is the purpose and the definition of the ego. Yet in our purifying consciousness, we see that this force is not offering us a better version of reality after all. For we do not feel better if after facing a loss of some kind, we become irritable and depressed. Although we know that these feelings will pass, we also know that they will come back again given similar circumstances.

What we are looking for is a way of responding to life-events that does not involve repeating these negative emotional responses over and over. The voice of Spirit says to us:

Trust in Me, for I watch over you at all times and shall make the way smooth for you, that you may join me in the Kingdom that awaits you.

Yet we see that our way is not yet smooth, and so we continue to face the choice of trust or mistrust in the voice of Spirit. This voice within the purifying consciousness tells us:

Your loss is not what it appears to be; it feels like a loss but its spiritual purpose is to bring to you something which you could not have acquired otherwise. For all losses are challenges that have concealed gifts within them—gifts of awareness and awakening.

Dear ones, the soul decides, depending on its awareness and its point in evolution, which voice to listen to. If it has made significant progress in attempts to purify, then the voice that it will listen to in this inner dialogue will be the voice of Spirit, howver painful that might feel. For the soul has begun to feel it cannot do otherwise. This is so because a degree of separation from the ego and its desires has already taken place, often over many lifetimes. As a result it has become easier for us to not attend to the inner voice which declaims against the Universe. For over time, we have come to believe in the perfection of life.

Beloveds, awareness of the perfection of all that is can happen in an instant, in a moment of revelation, but to integrate this awareness within the personality so that it serves at times of distress takes a much longer time. Realizing perfection is a process which occurs simultaneously with the process of purification, for how can we be impure or imperfect and see a perfect world? We approach both purification and the knowing of perfection by degrees, and as we approach these states we see them reflected outside of ourselves as well as inside.

It is not an intellectual understanding of perfection that is meant here, for that has been grasped long ago and was necessary to *begin* to walk the arduous path of purification. It is the actual experience of the perfection of the moment and of all moments to bring to us precisely what we need.

With purified vision, we are able to see more clearly that we have been given the gift of consciousness in order to fully appreciate the exquisite beauty and complexity of all events that surround us: the perceptual—through sight and sound; the intellectual—through information and understanding; the moral—through the awareness of universal and human law; the physical—through sensitivity to our own bodies and the actions of all bodies upon each other.

Through our human consciousness, we have been given an opportunity to experience the presence of Spirit through multiple channels of awareness. As we open to the center of our purity, we begin to notice that all that comes to us through the outer channels—the sights and sounds and words spoken to us, the speech heard on a radio serendipitously, or the song played on the radio of a passing car—in all of these we begin to notice a synchronicity of meaning. The events and images that surround us begin to testify to the truth that all life is ordered and interconnected through the inner meaning of experience. It is as if we were sitting in the middle of a symphony being played all around ourselves. All the harmonies are there, all the parts are listening to each other, and the director is nicely bringing together the different voices into a harmonious rhythm. This is the vision of perfection that comes to us as we purify and separate from the voice of the ego.

We are not lost or "out of synch" at any time of our lives really. We are always responding to and interacting with that universal flow of energy which has become personalized within our own lifestream. On the cosmic level it is referred to as the great Tao—the Way. Yet on the individual level we also have a *personal Tao*—which is the perfect movement of the energy patterns through our life (both inner and outer)—energy that will fully awaken the Divine being within.

Though our conscious minds may lose touch with this flow, the Tao does not lose touch with us. It is always guiding and pushing us toward the place of engagement with our destiny—the place where our personal Tao meets the Universal Tao and our personally felt purpose becomes identical with Divine purpose. This is the goal of all spiritual seeking and the purpose of our evolution within human form. It is a goal whose achievement will inevitably come to each of us, for whether we work toward it or not we are evolving in consciousness along with all other beings, and along with the planet which is our home.

Beloveds, what becomes possible at a certain point on our journey is to quicken the pace of this evolution through a more deliberate effort to purify, and through a more "faith-full" adherence to the knowledge of the perfection of all that is. As this becomes accomplished, we find that we no longer lose our equilibrium when events do not fit with conscious expectations, and we no longer define our feelings in the ordinary way as "happy" or "unhappy." We have chosen which master to serve, and the Light which calls us beckons us to live in peace and harmony. Therefore we are peaceful in the midst of turbulence, we are full in the midst of emptiness; and we are content in the midst of pain. All that comes to us is welcomed as part of the great perfection of life that moves through us and around us, and we know ourselves to be carried upon the great Waters by the same force that moved in the beginning.

"And the Spirit of God moved upon the face of the Waters. And God said, let there be Light; and there was Light."

PAX

To be a co-creator means that we must take responsibility for what we do with our thoughts, and consider which thought patterns we wish to energize. For this is the sacred trust we have been given, and a power beyond measure.

Chapter 14

And the First Shall be Last

Beloveds, the Mind of the One is the creator of the Universe. From the beginning of time It has woven out of the fabric of Divine energy and consciousness those forms that would benefit the balance of life within the solar system, upon the planet, and within the human organism itself. There is no living thing on this planet or within the Universe that was not conceived first as an idea within the Mind of Spirit. Each of us created in the image of God is part of this cosmic Mind; each of us has within this same power to create our world as does the Creator.

When we speak of the mind creating reality, we mean, literally, that what we think upon, clearly and continually, *becomes so*. This is because when we think, the mind sends out a stream of energy upon what is called the "mental plane" that creates, through the Law of Attraction, a magnetic polarization within the Universe. What we fear, expect, desire, or are preoccupied with is automatically attracted through the Law of Attraction, into our plane of experience. This might seem inconceivable to us if we did not each have the peculiar experience of having had things happen to us which could not be explained easily in any other way. For example: the precise person we wanted to meet shows up in a place or at a time when we would not have thought it possible. Or, what we fear most to happen, because it happened in our childhood, keeps recurring like a bad dream.

Beloveds, these "bad dreams" can be eliminated altogether from waking and sleeping life, by preventing our thought energy from vivifying what is undesirable.

Each of us is blessed with the power of that same spiritual energy that created the Universe, to create our lives. And ultimately we will all be co-Creators with the Divine Beloved, within our own personal lives and in the Universe as well. *To be a co-Creator means that we must take responsibility for what we do with our thoughts, and consider which thought patterns we wish to energize. For this is the sacred trust we have been given, and a power beyond measure.* Those who are completely able to regulate their thoughts are called Masters, and we will each be Masters one day.

One day we will realize that most of what we call "thinking" today—that steady stream of often inconsequential ideas and worries that moves through our daily lives—is not at all freely chosen, but rather comes to us *from the minds of others* who have taught us, raised us, and lived with us; it continues, in the present, to move through us from the minds of everyone around us.

In this sense we are all psychic and we are all telepathic. For the boundaries between one mind and another are permeable. This helps us participate in a common culture and have commonly held values. It helps us evolve into the highest pattern that that culture is capable of, by absorbing new ideas as they are spun out of the collective unconscious. Yet the limiting side of the permeability of mental boundaries must also be considered. For until we determine to *not* be influenced by the thought patterns of others, and to evaluate for ourselves the thoughts we think—until we literally ask of every idea that we hold: is this an idea that is worthy of a Divine being?—we will have little control over our mental lives, and consequently little control over those events that are brought into our lives through the patterning of our thought-energy.

Beloveds, we need to consider that thoughts are living beings with an energy of their own. And that even after they have passed through and out of our conscious minds, they are still active in the atmosphere around us, in our auras, and in the minds of anyone near us (physically or psychically) who has picked them up.

This is true on a planetary level, as well as on a personal one. The planet Earth is presently surrounded by an "astral belt" which consists of all the thought-forms that have existed in the collective conscious and unconscious minds of humanity that have been too "heavy" to rise to a higher plane of awareness. On this plane are thoughts borne out of ego-need and out of humanity's idea of itself as separate from God. And just as individuals can become embedded in a non-constructive thought process, based on the negative attitudes that they have learned, so too can the planet become embedded in a limiting and negative thought pattern, based on the ideas of those whose consciousness is part of the Earth's own.

Now that the Earth, including the "astral belt," is going through a process of purification, we are all being affected by these changes, and are being assisted in the purification of our thoughts. We can also choose to help in this cleansing process by taking responsiblity for what we release into the atmosphere around ourselves individually. In particular, thoughts of anger, injustice, greed, the desire for revenge, envy, superiority, etc. need to be replaced by thoughts of forgiveness, love, and compassion. As this becomes true on a personal and a planetary level, it will be for each as if the air had cleared. Everything will become simpler, plainer, and easier to deal with. And this is so be-

cause the light of the Spiritual Sun will be enabled to im-
bue the cleared consciousness of humanity with its truth
and joy.

Beloveds, the clearing and purification of the mind can
be done by each individual who chooses to open to the
light of Spirit. We need to ask that there be a healing
within the mind itself, so that those thoughts that are not
God-like can be distinguished from those thoughts that
are. In order to open our minds like this, it is necessary to
first adopt an attitude of true humility and non-judgment,
so that we are not attached to any particular thoughts that
have become part of our mental process. Then, in
humility, we may ask Spirit to impart that Divine insight
which distinguishes the true from the false, and the higher
from the lower. In order to prepare the way for the emer-
gence of the Divine voice—the I AM THAT I AM, it is
necessary first to purify the mind, so that the path is clear
and full of light. The hallmark of this attitude is seen in the
expression:

"Not my will but Thy will be done."

When an individual is willing to surrender judgments
that the ego has habitually made about situations to the
understanding of Spirit, he will begin to understand that
situation in a new way. If, however, that being chooses to
hold his own opinions and judgments to be *more important* than those of the inner Guide, he will bring to himself
repeated life-situations which will change these same
thought patterns, through the mechanism of karma, and
through interaction with the life-process itself.

Beloveds, it is not possible for consciousness to remain
at a static point in its development. We are always growing
and learning, and our thoughts, therefore, are always
changing. We can eliminate much pain and suffering from
our lives by allowing the grace of Spirit to move through

us. By being humble, and acknowledging our wish to express our oneness with Divine Mind, we become one with Truth, Goodness, and life itself. When we say to ourselves: *"Thy will be done,"* we allow a higher standard of judgment, based on God's supreme knowing to penetrate our ordinary minds, and we begin to see and feel things in a new, more loving light.

Beloveds, "the first shall be last and the last shall be first," has to do with the humility and *poverty of judgment* that we allow to be part of our consciousness, to make the way clear for Divine teaching within, and Divine inspiration. When we finally allow ourselves to let go of the idea that we must be *first* in our lives, in the sense of being superior, correct, winning, or proving ourselves to others in any way—but rather seek only to express what is within us without comparing ourselves to any other, we direct our attention to that Source of guidance within that can lead us to live fuller and happier lives. These lives are built not on competition with other beings, but on the joy that comes with full self-expression.

We have learned to desire being first because we have been ruled by the voice of the ego, and this is its message. In truth, there is no competition in our spiritual being and no failure: there is only learning. There is particularly no failure or inadequacy to be seen in relation to other human beings, for each is truly meant to follow her own unique path, and to experience and express the Divine voice within.

If we can begin to look at our lives through the eyes of Spirit, we can begin to judge our actions and thoughts solely by their intention to convey the highest Light that we are capable of. This purity of intention to reflect the Divine spark within in thought, word, and deed, leads more directly than competitive behavior or material achievement to the *feeling of success* and of *specialness* that we each long for. It leads to the sense of being filled, and

TEACHING THE HEART TO SING

fulfilled, in a way that material success does not. For success on the physical plane can and often does leave us with a feeling of inner emptiness which is then compensated for by a desire for greater success. While success in our relationship with God creates an inner sense of peace and of rightness that is always growing.

Let us therefore allow ourselves to be last in our need to judge others, situations around us, and ourselves. Let us ask to become part of Divine Mind—that Mind that inspired Buddha, Lao Tse, Confucius, Mary, Jesus, the prophets of old, and the wise beings of all ages, who were inspired in their wisdom through their surrender of the *conditioned mind* to the inspiration of the Divine. If we can be first in our desire to seek God's Truth and last in our desire "to be right," we will have taken a large step toward the purification of mind that leads to that holy sanctuary within which Spirit dwells.

PAX

To act in the consciousness of Love, even about the small things in one's day, recognizing all circumstances as coming from God and striving to feel the presence of the Divine Being while performing each action—this is to begin to live in the high state of consciousness that is naturally yours.

Chapter 15

The Sacred Heart

B eloveds, there is a sacred place within the human heart from which all truth and love emerges. It is the place of meeting of Spirit and Matter, and its entrance is concealed by the folds of selfishness and fear that often cover the heart. This dwelling place of Spirit has remained concealed from our knowing while we pursued the endless games of life, and the illusions of "maya" held sway over our individual and collective consciousness. As we unfold the petals of our heart's flowering through loving others, through living a dedicated life, and through a growing awareness of the true meaning of love, we open to a new perspective of selfhood—one in which we see that above and beyond all else—*we are love*. This quality of love that has at the center of our being is that same radiance that distinguishes saints and sages in every era, and that is part of us as well; it is love reflecting the heart of the Lord and Creator of all.

Beloveds, to become aware of love at our deepest core is not merely a matter of experiencing that emotion toward another being, though that experience sets the stage for what is to flower later on. Rather, it is a matter of reaching a point in our soul's journey where the primary question of

spiritual identity moves into the foreground of consciousness, and we begin to wonder about the qualities of a
Divine nature that are truly ourselves.

Within the inner chamber of the heart of each of us, hidden from ordinary vision, is the dwelling place of the
Divine flame which lights our being, and which causes us
to seek a deeper meaning in life and within ourselves
through successive lifetimes. As we begin the journey
within, our consciousness of who "I Am" becomes increasingly uncertain. We see more and more clearly that
who we are is a collection of labels that we have learned to
call ourselves that are rather temporary and transparent.
As we search for the true self, we learn to let go of these
labels in order to find that underlying essence that is the
object of our heart's yearning to know itself. Just as God
sought to know His God-ness by creating the diversity of
manifested life within form, so too do we each seek to
know ourselves and to see ourselves as we truly are. This is
the Divine gift of consciousness, and it belongs to each of
us.

Beloveds, let us knock on the door of spiritual awareness and ask to be let inside. The door is the door of our
hearts, and inside is the knowledge of being. Let us imagine going inside:

In the chamber of our heart we see a light, and within
the light a form.

We enter this illumined chamber and walk up to this
form:

"Who are you?" we ask.

"I Am the form of your Higher-Self," the form replies.

The form is more light than figure, with rays of energy
and light streaming from it. It continues to speak to us:

*"You have come to ask me about your true being, and I
will tell you:*

110

"All children of God have been created by the force of Love Itself, that force that forever connects your God-Self—the pure Spirit of your inner being—with the physical body and the personality it contains. There is no real separation between parts of your being, only separations in awareness. And just as you are aware of your toes and your fingers, the higher parts of your being are always aware of the lower; the lower, on the other hand, may have only a vague idea of the higher, though they seek always to live in harmony with what they feel as the presence of a guiding principle.

"Your Higher-Self loves you, and will always love you, for you are forever part of your God-Self, your individualized Spirit, just as you are forever part of the One—the I AM THAT I AM. At this level, dear ones these is only Love manifesting and expanding within the Universe, bringing into greater being the self-ness of all that is. This is how the Creator loved creation into being, and continues to do so. And this is how you are viewed as you blossom and flower.

"Dear ones, what we feel toward you is even more than the love of a parent for a child. It is more like the love of the artist for a work that has been inspired within him, in which, when it is completed, he sees the beauty of his own soul and experiences the presence of God.

"You, and other beings rising above the level of the personality, are taking the first steps toward overcoming the fear of loving, the fear of vulnerability, the fear of self-expression, the fear of being used or hurt by others. In order to protect yourselves, you have been careful about the amount you have allowed yourselves to love, and this was natural, since self-protection was a thought that many of you gave great credence to. In the present, dear ones, this thought is being replaced by the desire to be and to experience *all* that you are, and as universal energy moves through all levels of spiritual being, this desire will get stronger and stronger. Know this then:

"You are capable of a love that is limitless for each and every atom of the Universe. You are capable of love for the falling leaves, for the smell of grass, for sunlight and for stars, for every form—even for the instruments of technology which celebrate the bringing into form of a certain aspect of God's creative power. There is nothing in the Universe that cannot be loved *in its beingness* with this same love. Even materials and objects that have been created by man with a destructive potential, such as nuclear weapons, have, at their point of origin, the magic of Divine inspiration which allowed the energy within the atom to be correctly conceived of and harnessed. Man is meant to work with matter—to study and understand its principles. Therefore the victory of knowledge over the principles and uses of energy is and will be a great testimony to the intelligence and inspiration that reflects the Divine Mind within the human. In the mis-use of such energies, man makes further choices which are not part of their original purposes.

"In this arena as in others, dear ones, you must distinguish between your love for the presence of Spirit within the beings who imagined and created those techniques for harnessing nuclear power, and the ego-motivated behavior coming out of fear and competition, that subsequently led to their misuse. In this way, you can continue to see the Divine flow of the energy of Creation—an energy which continues to come to you even now in ever new forms of expression, and is distinct from the mis-appropriated use of this same Divine flow.

"All beings and all actions can be held in the consciousness of Love without exception, and as you release your judgments of what, to the human mind, may be considered *trivial* actions, you will begin to feel that each gesture that you make, however small, can be filled with the consciousness of Love that makes it significant—that makes it the best gesture of its kind and for its purpose that it can possibly be. In this sense, even the licking of a stamp, or the mailing of a letter, can be filled with the same amount of loving attention to the fullness of the moment, the meaning of the action, and the creative possibilities of the gesture, as any other act that you generally give more importance to.

"To act in the consciousness of Love, even about the small things in your day, recognizing all circumstances as coming from God, and striving to feel the presence of the Divine being while performing each action—this is to begin to live in the high state of consciousness that is naturally yours.

"Dear ones, the love that you are capable of has been called unconditional, and so it is, because it places no value on the outer appearance of its object, or on conditions that in human terms might limit its expression. It sees only Divine Being expressed within each form, and because of its Love for this Being, it is capable of embracing each form and each manifestation as Divine. **Be Love,** my dear one. That is your answer."

Let us imagine that the light-filled form within the inner chamber of the heart begins to fade with these last words, and only the sense of presence remains, and the words—**Be Love.**

Can we now open our hearts to this truth, in full understanding that we need no longer protect ourselves? *For what is there to protect ourselves from if all is One and all is God?* Even the pain of feeling hurt by another is also part of the experience of learning and of God. Can we open ourselves to this, *risking* more, that we may *learn* more of our true nature?

Within the sacred temple of our inner being lives the Divine flame of the I AM THAT I AM presence. We who yearn to be touched forever by the indwelling Spirit need to open our hearts more fully to love, until there is no fear in us and no resistance to its movement in our lives. There will be many places where we will continue to find judgment within ourselves, based on prejudice or world opinion or the feeling of fear. Yet the Christ within our hearts asks that *we* open the door and let His presence become manifest within our lives. Christ, the awareness of the Sonship and Daughtership, lives within the heart of each of us and is ready to emerge from behind the closed doors of unconsciousness, to be embraced by all who would see humanity change in the direction of Love. The Christ within calls to us, and as we are called to love God within all, we are asked to identify with Love that has always been there and to set it free.

Beloveds, the present moment *is* the time of the Sacred Heart, in which the Christ emerges from behind the doors where He has waited for millenia, to cast His radiance and Love upon all beings and to bless the Earth with the Light of Love that is the essence of His nature.

We who are willing to open to the presence of unconditional love are willing to hear this call *now*, are willing to take these risks *now*, despite the fact that our steps are uncertain and our beings not entirely free of fear. We who step forward into the Christlight are the stewards and saviors of the Earth, *and there are as many of us as there are beings who choose to open their hearts.*

Therefore let us welcome the truth of our being as Love, and let us rejoice that the new day that dawns for the planet will bring with it, through this opening within each of us, all that we have wished for of Divine Love made visible upon the Earth.

PAX

114

We cannot know where we are going, for we are in the process of going, and total involvement with our experience is necessary to take us to the next step of our development. Yet we can know that each soul, each being that we meet, has been around for millions of years, and that we are all learning from the experiences we have shared.

Chapter 16

The Moon Cycle and the Sun Cycle

In the history of pre-recorded time, there existed another solar system where ours now stands, and the energies of this system were fueled not by the star that we call our sun, but by that heavenly body that orbits the Earth— the moon.

The earlier moon "cycle" created a pattern of energies throughout the solar system that was very different from ours, and that had a different purpose. Through the ages of the Lunar cycle, a race of beings developed who were highly attuned to the lower astral and lower mental planes, and who had significantly developed the emotional side of their beings to the exclusion of other aspects. Over time, attraction to this level of consciousness could not let in enough light to further the processes of evolution. The Lunar Pitris, a name for the substance (matter and energy) of the lower astral and lower mental planes, crowded out the light of Spirit, and prevented the Earth from growing further on its evolutionary path. Eventually, both that race of humans and the solar system itself became extinguished.

Toward the end of this cycle, the ensouling Spirit of the solar system— the Solar Logos, determined to begin the creation of a new solar system, one that would more effectively represent the desire of Spirit to penetrate and spiritualize matter. The moon cycle came to an end when the "sun" of that solar system formed a supernova and extinguished. Souls that participated in Earth-school at that time had to wait millions of years for the next round of creation to build a suitable planet upon which they could take form. The Lunar Pitris of the astral and mental planes also dissolved upon the disruption of that solar system and returned to its primary energy form. Yet many of the souls that had been deeply affected by the lunar energy continued to carry it in the permanent atoms of being which remained at the soul level after death. These souls were therfore able to manifest "lunar" qualities upon entering the next cycle when a new solar system was born.

Much of what we consider to be the problem of accumulated karma operating on a world level today arises from this fact. For not only does humanity's *present* separation of consciousness from the Divine affect human actions; in addition, the presence of emotional residues from the earlier moon cycle continues to influence the auric fields of individuals who are given to expressing emotions of a low, self-seeking quality. These individuals form the people of the Earth who seem to continue to live primarily on the astral plane—activated by emotions of fear, greed, anger and lust, and their presence continues to build karma in the world.

From an evolutionary standpoint, it can be said that those areas of the world in which terrorism, manslaughter, assasination, genocide and other forms of highly charged negative emotionality prevail, are the areas where large groups of individuals are still heavily influenced by karma introduced during the moon cycle. These individuals are still carrying with them a fundamental need to activate the entire plane of violent emotions, inluding negative ones, in order to give new life to the Lunar Pitris. These individuals are not evil, nor are they lacking in Divine energy. They are as much individual sparks of God as are more "advanced" souls. But they have focused their energy at the lower astral level, because this is where they need to learn; *what* they need to learn is to progressively detach from the intense identification with this plane, and to move their energy to a higher level of consciousness.

The sun cycle we are presently in created a new solar system with a new purpose—one in which the *energy of mind* took precedence over the energy of emotion. Through the mind of the Solar Logos, the Spirit of the solar system, forms were created that could conduct the energy of Manas—the higher mental plane—so that beings could evolve to a higher stage of development. Emotionality still played a part in human evolution, but it did not play as great a part as it did in the Lunar cycle. Both the civilizations of Lemuria ·and Atlantis are part of this present cycle, and both expressed at their core different developments in the *use of mind* as a receiver and transmitter of Divine energy.

In Lemuria, mind was highly attuned to the forces of nature and to cosmic Spirit generally. Priests and priestesses, clairvoyants and healers were easily able to converse with the angelic realm, and with the Spirit of the Earth. It was a time of emphasizing the right-brain intelligence—a time which relied on intuition, inspiration, and Divine guidance.

In Atlantis, left-brain functions were emphasized, with the mind as creator and manifestor coming into the fore. A vast and awesome technology was created by Atlanteans which has not been duplicated to this date.

Both Lemuria and Atlantis, as well as our own civilization, have been instrumental in bringing us to the point where we now stand of needing to synthesize the best qualities of each civilization, and of the right and left- brain functions.

When we consider the pageant of recorded history, we see only a small segment of human life upon the Earth. In order to understand the true meaning of human history, we must learn to think of ourselves as timeless beings, existing long before recorded time. For challenges that we presently confront regarding the future of our planet are not just produced by the existence currently of nuclear energy, or the issues of capitalism and socialism. These are the modern ingredients of an ancient dilemma—that of understanding man's purpose upon the Earth. Technology, politics, economics, and history are *structural perspectives* or *grids* from which to view the changing aspect of our relationship to the Universe, and to our Divine being. With a longer view of where we have come from and where we are going, we may see ourselves more realistically.

At present, we are in the middle of a Solar cycle, and a spiritually attuned mind, including a blending or synthesis of right and left-brain functions—the goal of this present cycle—is only partly realized. Yet we have made great strides forward from the emphasis of the Lunar cycle, where only individual desire and need were viewed as the proper basis for the establishment of goals.

We cannot know where we are going, for we are in the process of going, and total involvement with our experience is necessary to take us to the next step of our development. Yet we can know that each soul, each being that we meet, has been around for millions of years, and that we are all learning from the experiences we have shared.

The moon cycle was for us a time of learning that led, on the spiritual level, to a new order of creation by those Intelligences that were respnsible for constructing the solar system. We continue to be part of a vast process of learning on all levels, and all Beings, including those whom we consider to be close to God, are also expanding in the process of learning and continued growth.

Let the moon in the sky remind us of an age that is past and of a light that has darkened, but that is still part of ourselves. As we keep the moon in view, let us bring our awareness to the memory of the Lunar cycle, and see that its Light and purpose had to be brought into balance with Divine purpose, so that the Earth as a planet, the solar system as a whole, and we as individuals within the Earth's body, might grow into the Divine Beings that we are.

PAX

For we are as eternal as the essence of the rose, and each moment of our lives has a particular quality that is equally unique and precious. Each moment, viewed from the standpoint of timelessness, has the jewel of the beautiful and the perfect within it—even within a prison, even with the prisons of our minds.

Chapter 17

The Way of Joy

Beloveds, there is no task more worthy of accomplishing than learning to live with an open and joy-filled heart, for in this way of living comes full empowerment to express the Divine within. Truly, there is no place or time when joy is not possible, for joy does not depend on outer circumstance at all for its existence, but rather is a condition of our being. It wells up from within like a fountain— ever-nourishing, ever-empowering. This is not a fountain of happiness or pleasure, so commonly mistaken for joy, for these feelings depend for their existence on the circumstances that produced them and will one day disappear. Happiness or pleasure are temporary, leading inevitably to the opposite feelings of sadness or disappointment as the conditions which produce these states come to an end. Joy, on the other hand, is a feeling of the Soul—based on the certainty that all is well and that there has truly never been anything to worry about.

Beloveds, *joy is produced by a sense of the timeless—it is connected with a deep realization of eternal being.* Whether this takes place in the presence of a sunset, or a flower, or one's child, or the truth within one's heart, joy sends its message of God's Love through the layers of the heart, to burst forth in the flowering of Truth. To live always in this state, what is needed is an ongoing sense of the timeless, and the assurance of eternal being.

It is possible to live in this way, dear ones, for the assurance of our eternal being, once found, can be held onto forever. No outer condition can threaten it in any way, no personal pain can touch it. Death itself has no power to alter the experience of joy, and for many may add to it.

To reach this fountain we have only to seek the timeless within any situation, and we are already there. Let us take, for example, a situation that would seem to be without joy, say that of a person living within a prison. We could ask, how can such a person live in joy? The answer, dear ones, is that the conscious experience of that individual need only be partly influenced by the restrictions which prevent the body from moving a certain distance beyond the cell, or the outer walls of a building. There *can be no restriction* upon the distance a soul can travel in realizing its own limitlessness. Therefore, in this situation as in others, the distinction between living as a body in the world and living as a Soul is basic to travelling through life in joy. As bodies, we are subject to the pain of limitation, of rejection, and of personal desire and frustration, and these pains can be quite severe at times. Each of us lives a life that has many great or small tragedies within it, for that is what it is to be human and to develop a heart of compassion. We live through these tragedies, and if we are open to life, we experience them deeply.

Yet there is a way in which joy can be present for us, even in the midst of sorrow, as we shift from the personal level of experiencing, *even in the midst of pain*, to the angelic or soul level. By doing this, we allow our hearts to sing in the midst of discomfort. We affirm our knowing that we have never left the angelic realm—that level of joyful vision that sees the human drama unfolding as a flower, beautiful and perfect. As angels we would never think as we watch a rose bloom that its beauty is limited by the fact

124

that it will one day wilt and die. Within our angelic vision, as we contemplate a rose, we simply do not see the limitations of its physical form at the time we are appreciating it. We drink deeply of its essence—its smell, its color, the softness of its petals, the way drops of dew cling to it in the morning sun. The life of a rose is short, but our *experience* of the perfection of that rose becomes part of what our souls most cherish.

In a similar way is it possible to view our daily lives in the light of timelessness, by constantly refocusing our attention as if we were looking at a flower. We do not need to focus on the limitations of that flower, and we do not need to focus on the limitations of our lives and define ourselves in those terms.

For we are as eternal as the essence of the rose, and each moment of our lives has a particular quality that is equally unique and precious. Each moment, viewed from the standpoint of timelessness, has the jewel of the beautiful and the perfect within it—even within a prison, even within the prisons of our minds.

If we could break down the limitations of our habitual thought patterns and see that what we often consider to be *more* important in the moment is the *less* important thing to look at, we could reveal a whole new way of living to ourselves. Our vision could become more deeply connected to the eternal, and our joy would spring from the deep knowing of this connection.

Some might hesitate in accepting this view, thinking that there are certain conditions in life that cannot be viewed in this way—situations that are too filled with pain. The death of one's child, for example, is an event which sears with the strongest emotions of despair, confusion, and anger, Beloveds, even in this circumstance, even in the midst of these human reactions, it is possible to know that the soul of one's child has given a gift of love that can never die, and that this gift has been shared and *will con-*

tinue to be shared, long past the death of the physical body.

If we can pull ourselves away from focusing on the limitations of the physical form that we inhabit—a form that is at best temporary and which must be cast off sooner or later—we can see that even at the time of death, the beauty and sanctity of love between two souls can far outweigh any other feeling that might be present in the situation. Other feelings need to be given inner space as well, but the timelessness of love in the presence of death can bring with it an experience of joy at the heart of spiritual knowing.

What is needed is a shift in perspective:

We walk in the country on an autumn day. We smell the air. We notice the trees. At one moment our minds are filled with the worries of the day and of our lives at that point in time. Yet in the making of this shift in perspective, we realize that these worries are all connected with the body and its happiness, and are not part of our eternal Self. What is part of eternity is our relationship with the Earth, with Light, and God's relationship with all that exists within form. If we raise our inner eyes from those concerns that burden us, we can see the timeless around us at each moment.

The dance of the sunlight and the trees is part of this timelessness; the gesture of slicing bread for a meal is part of this timelessness; the exercise of mowing the lawn or maintaining our home so that it is orderly and clean, can become a practice of creating beauty around ourselves so that we increasingly live in a state of harmony with our surroundings and with all that is.

The creation of harmony in our lives, whether through cleaning house, meditating upon God, taking care of our children, or writing a poem that expresses what we have set out to say—all these actions are expressions of our desire to live in harmony with life and can be part of the experience of the timeless.

What shall we say then of the absence of joy, the condition that many experience in their lives? The absence of joy, Beloveds, is produced by one thing alone: the lack of recognition that we are at all times souls, eternally held in God's Love, eternally safe. That this realm of experience— the human realm, the physical realm—is one that we have chosen to expand our soul's knowingness of the Divine. At each moment, joy can come from asking what God wishes us to see *now*. If we look, we will always see it—for the gifts of Spirit are everywhere, only obscured by our focusing on limitation, rather than on beauty, harmony, or love.

Dear ones, the joyful experience of life is one to which we are being called, for it is our true nature to experience joy at the core of our being. This does not mean that sadness and difficulty *will not* also be part of our experience. For on the path homeward, there are inevitably lifetimes and periods within one lifetime when the soul's learning accelerates and greater mastery is achieved through greater challenge. This is always the soul's choice and many of us have chosen lives of great difficulty in order to learn more quickly of our Divine nature. We have therefore asked Spirit to bring all areas of darkness and misconception into the Light of our awareness.

This call to Spirit will *always* be answered. For God does not deny Her children the satisfaction of their desire to return Home. And so as we become more impatient in our efforts to purify ourselves—that we may return to that Home which we know awaits us—difficulties in our lives will present themselves at times, letting us know where we have yet to change and grow. And in the midst of these challenges joy can be our companion and our friend. We can invite joy to walk with us through the fields of limitation, through the "valley of the shadow of death," knowing that we see only *shadows* of limitation. Let us remember that the Eternal One is within us, is our innermost nature, and that we will inevitably be reunited with this, our true Self, in consciousness and in love.

And the Lord said to the people of Israel, arise and go forth into the land of milk and honey, and let my Voice be thy guide, and let My hand be thy protection.

For from this day forth let it be known that the children of God live in the land of the Eternal One, and shall be nourished by the heart of that One, and fed by the light of His love. And God spake thus to the children of Israel as they crossed the great desert.

And it was so.

PAX

To live creatively is to die each day to the old and to make way for the new in oneself, for the potential self that is waiting to be born. It is to be willing to constantly release assumptions about what we should *be doing, or where our lives* should *be going, and to live in a state of wonder as a young child asking: who will I be today?*

Chapter 18

Death is Not Forever

Beloveds, the consciousness of the sacred teaches us that there is only life everywhere around us—that nothing is merely form. This is equally true of the event we refer to as death, which needs to be viewed as a bridge through time into another phase of our life. Just as birth is a bridge from worlds forgotten or only dimly remembered, so too is death a transition of equal proportions—a return to the awareness of the eternal and a leaving of the world of the transient. In death we are offered a new opportunity for growth, not only at the time of dying, but afterward as well as our Spirit leaves our physical form and travels onward to a place of new learning.

All of life as we know it would be altered by our willingess to face death at each moment. We would see fear and avoidance disappear as all beings became empowered to express their deeper selves. For the fear of death keeps many from taking those risks that would add to life the fullness of encounter in which true learning takes place. These risks exist on all levels— physical, mental, emotional, and spiritual. They are the risks of letting go of the familiar, and moving into an area that is at first totally unknown, and therefore totally uncertain.

Each naked encounter with the unknown, on whatever

level it occurs, and each letting go of the security of the familiar, produces an encounter with death. In a sense, we die to who we have been up until that moment and allow ourselves to become something that is yet unseen. These mini-deaths are reflections of an openness to life that needs to be ongoing. Wherever we are and in whatever task we find ourselves, we can live on the edge of the known, striving to find the new frontier of learning within ourselves—or we can live within the familiar, maintaining our sense of security as long as possible.

The experience of sudden tragedy or pain confronts many of us with a knowledge of death even where there is no actual dying. At these times, we are faced with the unpredictability of life, which draws from us a response we could in no way have foreseen. In the face of extreme change within our lives, or extreme loss, we are thrown up against our fundamental attitudes toward the *changingness of life itself* which we may have hidden from.

The process of physical death is but an extension of these smaller deaths that occur throughout our lives, that bring us in touch with the knowing that nothing in life is absolutely certain or absolutely solid. For life itself is just the flow of energy moving inexorably toward an unseen goal. When we cannot trust this flow, we are carried by the current of life and struggle to move against it in fear of getting overturned or of drowning. In resisting, we toss and turn and in the process we hurt ourselves. Trusting the current, we experience a smoother ride, for we let go of the need to see what lies ahead and like a raft floating dowstream, we ride the current till it opens out at its destination.

As individuals and as a people, it is time for us to recognize our collective fear of the unknown and the ways in which decisions to avoid un- knowingess limit the creativity of our lives. Social and political structures and the histories of entire nations have been based on this fear, and the attempt to stabilize change. This is equally true within individual lives where outer circumstance pleads with us for a revision of our life-positions, and where often we refuse out of fear to make the required shift. This applies to changes in career choices, in relationships, in daily rhythms, and in our view of ourselves. We hold onto what is familiar as if it were true *because* it is familiar.

Dying within life brings to each of us an opportunity to stretch ourselves further than we have ever dreamed possible; as we die to the idea of the self that we were, or thought we were, a new self emerges with qualities that surprise us. This new self was always present within us, yet was awaiting the proper time in the drama of our life to enter and play its part. The emerging self is not a part of us that is already formed, but rather a part that exists as a potentiality within us, a bud, that has waited for the correct conditions in the internal and external environment to make its appearance. In a sense it is a potential self that has lived through a long gestation period, entirely comparable to the physical embodiment of this same process. As the internal psychic and spiritual conditions nourish it, it eventually finds a way to get born into the light of manifestation.

To live creatively is to die each day to the old and to make way for the new in oneself, for the potential self waiting to be born. It is to be willing to constantly release assumptions about what we *should* be doing or where our lives *should* be going, and to live in a state of wonder as a young child asking, who will I be today?

Living without a fixed identity is a *feeling state*, a state of readiness for the unknown to enter and change us. In fact, there are many aspects of the structure of our lives that continue, for there are relationships that fulfill our duty or purpose in life, and there are areas of activity chosen by each soul that allow the greatest amount of learning to take place. The fluidity of the individual self-concept can exist within any structure or form, and is not dependent on these. This fluidity depends only on our willingness to have the current of life move us to the next step of our unfoldment—to ride the current and let it carry us downstream.

Only faith can sustain us in this position—faith in the ultimate beneficence of the Universe and of God. Yet beloveds, there is a paradox here that will be experienced by those who attempt to open to death within life — that faith does not need to be present *except in small degree* as we release in trust to the unknown. The *experience of releasing* and of saying "in Thee will I trust" has the effect of *producing* the faith that is necessary to sustain us on our journey. For once we let go of security, we are buoyed up by a process that is actually quite natural to us and that we may begin to recall we have practiced before. For we have, in countless lifetimes, practiced the experience of dying, and letting go in trust to this death. For some of us this may apply primarily to the experience of leaving the physical body, repeated over many incarnations. On some level the soul remembers that this bridge has been crossed, and that when we release into trust we tap into this experience of letting go more and more deeply. Yet it is also true that for many, these prior experiences may have involved trauma, fear, or pain of a particular kind. Therefore the present experience of letting go and dying to the known either physically or psychologically requires our loving attention in order to heal the specific anxiety that may have been aroused.

This practice of healing our fear of dying can occur every day of our life if we allow it to. It can occur through recognizing our fear of the unknown— our fear of change, of being ourselves, of dropping external standards that serve to validate who we are. As we do this with our children, at work, with our partners, in play, in sexual expression, and in the physical challenges we face—we heal the fear of dying. As we responsibly face each decision that we make by seeing what identity we are affirming in our choice, what concept of self we are upholding, and peek around the corner into the darker spaces of our minds to see what view of ourself we might be avoiding, we come face to face with the unknown. For there is always this choice in decision-making—to remain true to who we are at the moment, as defined by how we have acted up until now on the stage of our personal dramas, or to see who we might be in the next act.

We are always becoming someone new.

The truth of the potential that we share to become per-petually new, to be born each day or in each moment, is one we face most significantly at the time of leaving the physical body. For it is at that time that we face what seems to be the greatest amount of un-knowness—life out-side the body, life apart from the familiar faces and rela-tionships that have formed part of our identity—and life apart from the personality we have just been.

The movement across the bridge of the physical dying process can be made easier for us if we have already faced the experience of death within life. Then, openness to the new at the time of dying becomes an extension of what has already opened up within us—trust, confident expecta-tion, and a yearning to embrace life. Death of the physical body can be greeted from this perspective with joy, for it releases the soul from the planes of matter where great learning has taken place, to the planes of spiritual being where learning and life will continue.

What is needed at the time of death is an environment in which we are surrounded by others who support us on our continuing journey into the new. Ancient cultures created beautiful and sacred rituals designed for this purpose, which included a gathering of the community. Deathchants, prayers, poems, and sacred dances were part of the celebration—all that would aid the dying person in her desire to connect with the sacred meaning of her death. We need to return to this communal celebration, especially at the time of death of a loved one. Then, most of all do we need to find the proper means for assisting that one in the expansion of trust as she crosses the bridge into the unknown. As we support the dying of a loved one in this way, we also support each other in our own dying, and reduce the remaining fear of letting go that continues to live within us.

This loving support within our personal milieu, as well as within humanity as a whole, is greatly needed at a time when many struggle on spiritual as well as physical levels to release their identification with the body. We are souls, and at the time of death we encounter a part of the human experience that we have chosen as souls in order to learn about the true nature of our relationship with God. As we continue to see human suffering and tragedy occurring in the world around us, as we witness the death of countless individuals through poverty and starvation, through war or political repression, through alcohol and drugs, through AIDS or another widespread diseases, we need to maintain a perspective about the meaning of these experiences that will allow us to continue our lives in trust, rather than in fear or despair.

Let us know then that the conditions of dying are chosen by each soul prior to coming into the physical body. The conditions of dying form part of the same energy flow that is part of the karma and of the healing that each of us *needs to experience* for our growth. Beloveds, this is true without exception: we cannot judge from either the conditions of dying or the suffering of the individual being, what the inner process of dying may actually be like. We cannot know, except through contact on a soul-level, what that soul might be learning, moment by moment, as it releases its hold on the physical body. Though we need to feel compassion for the human suffering that each being experiences on the physical level, and seek to reduce that as much as possible, we must at the same time release judgment regarding the rightness of that pain if we are to maintain our own trust in life.

Each soul is the judge of its own experience while living and while dying, just as each soul is the creator of that experience. Let us learn to help each other face the encounters with life and death that we have created for ourselves with courage, with honesty, and with deep appreciation of the hidden beauty that can transform even the moment of greatest suffering into a significant encounter with the Divine. Let this be our gift to the dying and our gift to ourselves as we die—that we ask to encounter the Divine at each moment of death, realizing that there is no ending in life, no true death at all:

There is only the ongoingness of the stream.

PAX

If we want to know who we are and what we are capable of, we need to look into the future *of ourselves and of humanity, as well as the past, for that future is now within us.*

Chapter 19

Awakening From the Dream

Beloveds, as we awaken from the limited sense of our identity as creatures of the physical plane, and take in more and more of the truth of our eternal being, we realize that the structures of space and time we live in are human dimensions, and that we needed these when we could no longer perceive the eternal through our senses. These structures tell us that we live in a linear dimension, that we begin and end. And whether we conceive of this beginning and ending within one life-cycle or over successive reincarnational cycles, we still view ourselves as creatures whose growth depends on time.

Beloveds, this is only partly true. It *is* true that the language of *karma* and *reincarnation* that we use speaks to us in concepts that are defined by the dimension of time—by the relationship of what we call the "past" to what we call the "present." Yet this language, while valid at its own level, can be limiting for us when it prevents us from discovering the greater truth of our unfoldment as beings outside the linear time dimension that we are familiar with. In our beingness, we are *all stages of ourselves simultaneously*.

In this broader view, karma reflects the harmonizing and balancing power of God, the Life-Force, as It brings into greater wholeness all aspects of the expression of our being. It is as if each lifetime were a note in a magnificent and complex chord; though we ordinarily experience the notes separately and hear them separately, they are all being played together. Karma in this sense, is the Divine Director of the symphony—harmonizing all notes in the chord, and relating our chord to all other chords in the great song of being.

To see this more clearly let us think of a flower. When we think of a flower we may first picture its beauty in bloom, and certainly when we draw it this would be likely. But our concept of "flower" includes: budding, blooming, fading, falling, and dying all within the same idea. In a similar fashion, we too have been created as living transformative images in the Mind of God—each image a part of our wholeness—each united with all others in Divine Mind. As Divine images, we are not limited by the cycles of time except within our own consciousness. And if we could see ourselves from the perspective of the eternal as God does, we would see what runs through the successive stages of our unfoldment is our essential quality—our "flowerness." At every point in our human "history" we are expressing this essence.

If we were to take a photograph of the same object from a number of different perspectives—seeing it now this way, now that, in a myriad of lights and views, and if we were then to align these photographs so that we could see all views simultaneously, we would be viewing this essence—the harmonic "note" or "chord" of our inner being. This is the vision of us which God sees in the eternal present—the perspective from which all embodiments and all forms that we have created are seen as expressions of the same underlying spiritual reality.

From the standpoint of the concrete mind, we experience ourselves as living through one view or one photographic frame at a time, rather than sensing the inner creative core of our being from which the whole show emanates. We use time to organize our thoughts and our lives—to help us explain the appearance of certain events based on the appearance of other events preceding them. Time is a structure of thought which is useful in the ordering of life, when the rational mind or ego feels the need to be in control. Yet we might consider at this time that we are outgrowing this need to some degree, and that we can rethink our whole relationship to the temporal.

Let us consider that what we hold to be *successive* lifetimes of incarnation, linked together through the eternal presence of the Soul and through Law of Karma, is actually a more complex arrangement or energy flow. This flow weaves through all stages of our unfoldment—past, present, and future, bringing them all into harmony with each other.

The view of ourselves through time is not an incorrect one, Beloveds, but it limits our consciousness from appreciating the wholeness of life that may be available to us as we reconceive of who we truly are. For it is not just the past which influences our present behavior—not the past within this life or our reincarnational "past." It is also the "future" which influences our present behavior, the future that already exists within us. What we call the "future" is another frame or view within which our essential self unfolds, and the time of its occurrence is *now*.

The sense of limitation created by our thinking of who we *have been* places great burdens upon our imaginations as we look at the circumstances we have come from personally, in terms of our family heritage, or collectively, in terms of the history of mankind. Looking at our past, we are taught to believe that we are limited by conditions of our heritage on whatever level we imagine it. Nothing is further from the truth.

If we want to know who we are and what we are capable of, we need to look into the future of ourselves and of humanity, as well as the past, for that future is now within us.

It can be found by releasing concepts of the "possible" and "impossible," and by allowing ourselves to have a vision of what our heart aspires to when it is most open. This attunement to the future is more than a wish. Perhaps it will only be expressed as a wish *in this lifetime*, but if that is the case, it will be because the individual holding that wish believes that it is a wish, and not truly his Self.

Beloveds, any heartfelt image of the self that we can conceive is *already* us. Within some other view of our personal reality than what our present personality is expressing, we have already been that, or will become that.

These words "have been" and "become," again express a language-form which continues to reflect the time-dimension that we order our lives with. What is more true to say is that we *are already* manifesting, at some other level of reality, anything that we conceive ourselves to be at this level. This is the nature of thought, to create its own reality. This is the nature of Divine purpose for humanity—that we be fully able to express and experience all reflections of our Divine being within a diversity of forms.

Images of limitation can be easily overcome Beloveds, if we realize that we are influenced by our past only to the degree that we believe ourselves to be. Whatever "karmic influence" may be affecting our life in the present will be operative only as long as that influence remains not fully conscious within us—an unhealed part of ourselves. When we release that thought from our identity—release it to the *future* possibility of a Self which no longer holds that particular karmic influence, then we have freed ourselves from that karma.

The true difficulty in doing this is the difficulty of becoming fully conscious of what we really think, for what we speak of as karmic influences operate on the deepest psychological level. Their purpose is to enable us to integrate all aspects of our being at higher and higher levels of spiritual integration. If we can become conscious of and release our identification with the whole pattern which karma is bringing up, and hold it against the pattern of a future self that we *believe is true*, karma will have achieved its beneficial purpose more quickly, through the power of thought.

This, Beloveds, is the goal of Mastership—to be able to sufficiently clear the mind so that all thoughts become conscious as they occur, and can be regulated according to what is desirable to create. It is also the foundation for the operation of Divine Grace within our lives—that flow of energy which comes from being in harmony with the pattern of our Divine image and purpose. Only the limiting and negative thoughts that we hold about ourselves can diminish the full presence of Grace in our lives, and we can bring Divine Grace into play more and more as we focus on the nature of our consciousness. In this way, we discover that we are not who we thought ourselves to be, and that we do not have to continue to be limited by any belief we hold.

The secret, Beloveds, is consciousness, and an identification with the full potentiality of our being. We are flowers-in-the-process-of-unfolding, and all stages of this unfoldment occur simultaneously. The Hopi Indians knew this, as have other ancient cultures, and created a language in which there were no nouns representing things, but only verbs reflecting ongoingness and change. This is the direction that we each must travel in, and it will create much joy in our lives as we learn to recognize the limitlessness of what we can create. We can soar, Beloveds, to places that we have never dared dream of that are possible of realization *now*.

Awaken, awaken!

PAX

When the Divine flame within the atom, the sacred Fire, becomes connected to the flame within the heart, and to the regulating centers within the human brain, at that point man becomes a Master of the material world.

Chapter 20

The Flame of the Divine

The root of all energy within matter is the essence that is called the Sacred Fire—that which transforms the inert atom into a vital living thing. This Fire, also a form of Electricity, is a force that pervades the Universe from the tiniest of atoms to entire galaxies. It is not to be considered merely electrical force in the sense that the physical plane defines this term, for it is much vaster and more powerful than that. Yet its purpose, on a spiritual level, is the same—to create an animating current between polarities that hold, through the force of attraction, the impulses existing between them. Therefore, within the atom and within the Universe there will always be a positive and a negative pole of attraction to which all forms of matter will be drawn at different times. The presence of Sacred Fire, or Fohat, may be considered to be the building block or cement of the manifested Universe, and its creation is ongoing.

The physically manifested Universe is continually being created through the mental process spun out of the Mind of God, through that same Mind that lives within all lesser minds, including the human. Vast Intelligences within the Universe are employed in creating, through the conscious use of the Sacred Fire, whole realms of being in a similar fashion to that process by which an individual human being is capable of creating her own life. Through the mastery of the use of sacred Fire, humanity can become a co-creator with these Intelligences and with the One Spirit pervading all.

When the Divine flame within the atom, the Sacred Fire, becomes connected to the flame within the heart and to the regulating centers within the human brain, at that point man becomes a Master of the material world.

Preceding this is a long period of necessary training in appreciating the power of thought to affect life. This is essential in understanding the true relationship between thought and energy. By sending out a clear current of thought, amplified through the heart and head centers, we can tap into that energy which exists within the physical atom as Fire or Electricity; and by directing thought, we can transform its potential from a particular expression within form that it now holds, into another form, or back into formless energy.

The potential to transform matter into energy is already known by scientists, and the process by which energy can be transformed back into matter will also become familiar in the not too distant future. Yet for each of us, the true need at this moment is to understand the power existing in raw form throughout the Universe—energy to be harnessed by technology, and more importantly, by our human thought. Energy that can be put to uses that can further the highest development of mankind, or that can destroy much of what civilization has achieved.

We are each capable, even at this point in our development, of harnessing this pure energy to some degree, simply by determining that we will *act* and *think* as if we *already* were capable of creating life and form in this way. This means the clear designation of a purpose and goal to which we can commit ourselves, and the elimination from consciousness of all doubt that stands in the way of this commitment. The purpose of dedicating ourselves to the attainment of specific goals is that it focuses, in a rudimentary way, the alignment of our heart center, our head centers, and the sacred Fire in surrounding matter, so that we can begin the process of alignment of the material world with the mental.

The process by which many today have aligned themselves to contemplate and reflect upon world peace at the same time all over the world, and what we are discussing here, is identical. It is the process by which minds collectively focus the energy of thought to influence both the mental plane—affecting the minds of others—and the material plane. In the latter case, the energy of the physical atoms themselves becomes influenced by the collective thought pattern that emerges.

These meditative exercises are useful in transforming the Earth, but of even greater usefulness is the way in which each of us chooses to live our daily lives. For the thoughts emanating from the ordinary process of living have more weight, due to their frequency and often to their emotional power, than the thoughts which can be focused during a brief meditation. The thoughts that we think moment-to-moment need to increasingly reflect our understanding of the relationship betwen the mental and the material. We can, if we choose, literally change the physical environment around us by deliberately conquering self-doubt, fear, and mistrust, and by projecting our intentions clearly at all times in terms of what we wish to create. Over time, this attunement begins to bring into alignment the energy of our head and heart centers, and we begin to actually experience a taste of that Divine power that is naturally ours.

Power or energy can now, as it has in the past, be misused for selfish purposes, for the Sacred Fire is neutral and will adapt itself to any force that knows how to regulate it, for better or worse. What must be understood, dear ones, is that if we were to experiment with mental energy and matter in ways that were harmful to ourselves or others, these experiments would eventually backfire. *For although energy is neutral, the Law of Love is not.* The Law of Love is that which lies behind the mechanism of Karma within the Universe, and that Law would require the healing of the thought pattern within the individual that trespassed on the rights of others.

Therefore, in looking at the operation of the mind in relation to the Sacred Fire, it is vital that we always ask if what we are wishing to create serves our highest good, and the highest good of others who might be affected. There is no point and no value in attempting to create what is not in harmony with Divine Will. For through the Law of Love, anything that we create that does not express the divinity within us will at one time or another need to be brought into harmony with the Divine, through the balancing action of karma and healing.

Fohat or Sacred Fire, is an element that Spirit has given to us that we may celebrate in freedom and in joy the fact of our heritage as children of God. At present, advanced development of skills in this area have often been used to amuse or entertain others, such as in the practice of bending spoons or in the practice of telekinesis. These are small, concrete examples of what can be done through a mind that focuses and that believes itself to be a transmitter of energy.

In aligning ourselves with the Sacred Fire, we must properly link up the Divine flame within the heart with the mind and the body. For the mind can be saying one thing in terms of intention, while the heart says another. In order to influence the energy within matter, *heart and head must be aligned without conflicting motives, purposes, or feelings.* That is why it is much easier to manifest simple concrete things in our lives, for simple things do not as frequently produce the conflict between heart and head that interferes with this entire process.

Over time, as the desire nature of each of us purifies and we become more and more accustomed to trusting our Divine knowing, it will become easier to link the heart and head. But for the present, what is useful is to spend a little time each day in search of alignment, registering all levels of motive and feeling that might exist within our hearts when a particular outcome is desired, so those that are the most difficult to remove at least come into the light of consciousness.

What is not conscious cannot be changed, Beloveds, for all change comes through a change in consciousness and rarely does this happen without the conscious mind being involved to some degree. Therefore, by examining the motives of our hearts at all levels, we can work with conflict in order to dispel it. We can examine the inner attitudes that foster the attainment of what we desire, and turn over to Spirit those that are legacies of the past and that are not constructive. Initiation of this healing process, whenever a goal that has not materialized is still being pursued, is of utmost importance, for there is truly no area in which we are not capable of creating our own lives.

At the same time, we must know that a complex goal, one that involves a change in *all* aspects of our life, may take a long time to manifest, and therefore the healing process necessary to create the head-heart alignment may be long and intense, producing outer changes that may create distress for us, rather than appearing as a simple and clear step-by-step approach to our goal.

Beloveds, we need to bear in mind that the process of healing through the Law of Love is always taking place. If we have created a clear goal within our hearts and minds that we wish our life to manifest, and if we have examined our hearts, asking that all motives be brought to the light of spiritual awareness, we must assume that outer circumstances, painful or pleasant, are bringing us closer and closer to the realization of that goal.

In God's presence we live, move, and have our being. By activating that Presence within us, we become one with the purpose for which we have been created. In this way we begin to discover that limitlessness and greatness that is ours, within the specific reality that we have chosen in the present.

PAX

PART III: *Love*

The reason that you have walked in darkness, through the winding tunnels of love, is not to create fear in you or to punish you. It is to make you stronger in your willingness to seek the Light...

Chapter 21

The Pathways of Love

"Lord," speaks our soul, "the pathways of love are winding, leading us through a maze of tunnels in semi-darkness. We hug the walls as we walk, unsure of our direction, unsure of which turn to take when the path curves—a sudden corner here, another corner there—which way do we go?

"Lord, we look for the Light, but do not see it directly ahead—yet just enough light is before us so we know there must be an end to the darkness of the tunnel. We become afraid, and we begin to pray:

"Lord, lead us out of darknesss into Light. For Thou art the good Shepherd.

"We recite: *The Lord is my Shepherd, I shall not want.*
He maketh me to lie down in green pastures,
He leadeth me beside still waters.
He restoreth my soul...

"Lord," we call out. "Restore us. Bring us peace."

We manage somehow to maneuver through these tunnels of fear and doubt and pain that suddenly appear in our lives. When what was expected disappoints us we feel the loss. We feel the grief. How could we not? And we try again and again to explain this to ourselves.

"Lord," speaks our soul. "Have I done something wrong? Is that why this loss has come into my life? Have I failed Thee? Am I being punished? Is it true Thou art a wrathful God? I had not believed it Lord, but is it true? Tell me, I need to know why this has happened to me. Why do I walk in darkness and alone, when You said You would be here with me?

"My child," says the Lord.

"My beloved child. I have never left you. I have never abandoned you. For you are my own—you are forever within my heart.

"The reason that you have walked in darkness, through the winding tunnels of love is not to create fear in you or to punish you. It is to make you stronger in your willingness to seek the Light, to purify and test you so that your decisions will never again be based on fear, but rather on the determination to seek the Truth and Love that you know is possible.

"My child, my dear child, you had settled for so little in your life because you had lost the vision of what was possible. You chose the path of least resistance, remaining with the things that gave you comfort—the reassurance of others, the security of the familiar, and the half-hearted accomplishment of a task that if accomplished well would have revealed your great beauty to you. Therefore my child, I lead you through these pathways of darkness so that you will know your own strength, and your willingness to persevere in seeking Truth. For the tunnel of darkness, my child, is a metaphor for your inner un-knowing of the voice that speaks of Me and My love for you. It is the outer form of your inner uncertainty.

"Let go my child, of this mistrust, and you will begin to see the Light streaming through the darkness."

"Lord, You ask me to trust You, yet as I stumble through these halls of darkness, I cannot see where to put my feet, and there is no one here to guide me. Why do You not appear to show me the way? If it is a matter of learning to trust my strength, why do You not give me work that I can do to become stronger; of what value is this experience of being lost in this tunnel and not knowing which way to turn?"

"My child, it is because your strength needs to be sheathed in the scabbard of faith, and your Light needs to be protected by the shield of holy purpose that I ask this. As you go this way and that, trying to find your way, you bring together your mind, body, and Spirit into one common purpose— to find that which you are looking for. And since you have no guide, you must rely on your inner Guide, which is all that any child of God has ever needed. Rely then on your inner Guide, my child, and let it tell you whether there is a need for concern in the darkness."

"Lord. I do not know where I go, and I do not know what lies ahead of me. I only know that I love You and that I seek to love and serve You. Teach me to hear the guidance within me, that I may find my way to You. Show me the passageway Home, Lord, for I am tired of wandering through darkness and seek only You."

. . . And the Lord said to the people of Israel:

"Out of the valley of bondage will I deliver my children, when their longing for Me has ripened; I will deliver them from the hand of the Pharoah. Instead of serving an unjust

ruler, they shall find renewed freedom in Me. And I shall lead them through the desert into barren lands, that they may learn to trust God within the desert, and to know always that they are safe within My hands.

And into that desert—that land of unknowing, shall come the light of Love and Truth to purify the minds and bodies of those who seek Me in faith; and they shall be unto me as my right hand and the inner part of my heart, for they shall know their oneness with Me and with the Kingdom that awaits them.

This glory do I bestow upon those who seek Me in darkness and unknowing, for their faith is their strength, and their persistence is their love for Me, and the prayer in their hearts is the voice of their Souls."

And the people of Israel travelled through the desert to a place of beauty called Sinai, and peace came upon the land.

PAX

When there are no more strangers for us in the world, when we see each other as brothers and sisters, then the heart can open fully to the day and to all events within it, for there is no one left to fear, and no one left to judge. There is only love to be re-discovered.

Chapter 22

The Brotherhood of Souls

Beloveds, from time immemorial souls have travelled to the Earth in pairs, in families, and in groups in order to more effectively support each other's work and growth on the Earth plane.

This brotherhood/sisterhood of souls gives rise to what is now so commonly experienced on the physical plane as the sudden meeting up with one of these group or family members, and the recognition almost instantaneously that we have known this other, this stranger, for a very long time. This is the truth, Beloveds, for as each of us becomes more sensitive to the rays of higher energy coming from outer sources as well as inner, there is bound to be greater recognition, based on *resonance* with another. This phenomenon takes place on an energy level, not on an informational or practical level. It is therefore often not necessary to know a lot about one with whom we have this feeling of familiarity and of likeness. We simply know this person at what we feel to be a deep inner level of their being, and we must learn to believe in the truth of this knowing.

There are many soul-mates for each person in the sense that I am speaking of. There are many who have, through successive incarnations, been with each other as brothers, mothers, husbands, friends, and even adversaries. We come into each other's lives at prearranged times, in terms of where the energy pattern of our life has taken us—and when the stage is set, the soul with whom we have agreed to share our growth and learning appears. This does not always refer to a life-partner appearing at a specific time in our life, for a life-partner is but one of the many kinds of soulmates that we have in any given life. A beloved friend, a teacher—anyone with whom we have a significant relationship especially of a transformative kind, can come into our lives in order to help us with a particular facet of our growth. And their longevity within our lives, say in the case of a lover or partner, has no bearing on the reality of the spiritual relationship or its importance.

We are all part of a great soul community or network, and each of us is linked up with all others to different degrees. For we have all been together over time and have had thousands if not millions of opportunities to exchange energy with other souls in countless incarnations. This energy exchange is the basis for later familiarity.

Beloveds, recognition of this fact will lead to greater openness and greater trust in the "accidental" meetings we might have in the course of a day, for no meeting is truly accidental, and the person we bump into "accidentally" in the supermarket, at the library, or in a store, may be instrumental in catalyzing for us, in some small way, a turning point in our lives—a choice between one path or another. This can happen either by their delivering a "message" to us that we have needed to hear—a message that perhaps can be heard more easily from a stranger—or by their simply affecting our energy field with their own vibration. We can have no way of knowing how these seemingly incidental brushes with strangers influence our lives, until we know through the *experienced reality* that there are no strangers, that each and every person we meet is related to us in some way. When we truly understand this, we will not be surprised by or minimize the small encounters that are life-changing, and we will more deeply appreciate the larger ones, whether they seemed to have helped us at the time or not.

The souls of our spiritual family are a special group that differ from the souls of our physical family. The souls of our spiritual family share a common resonance, a pattern of energy that defines a common soul-purpose or essential quality, and a common path on an inner level in relating to God. The souls of our spiritual family may not appear on the surface to be similar to ourselves. Their occupations, lifestyles, personalities, choice of friends, interests, etc. may all differ. Yet in their presence there is a sense of peace and harmony, as if we had finally come home. This perception comes from the quality of *resonance* which takes place on an energy level when we feel *known* and appreciated. Beings within a spiritual family have what may be called a "group soul," as well as an individual soul. Throughout time, they have as a group defined a specific purpose or energy pattern that they wish to achieve or manifest. And much as the individual soul, throughout the course of its evolution, seeks to manifest its own highest expression of divinity, so too does the group seek to manifest the highest expression of the soul-quality it shares with all members of that group. These soul qualities may express in the realm of artistic endeavor, politics and leadership, poetry or music, religious devotion. In any area, members of a spiritual family assist one another in their efforts to realize God through the expression within form of their highest soul qualities.

Organizations and formal groupings may have little to do with family membership on a spiritual level, even where the organization itself is a spiritual organzation. Some members of an important group in our lives are likely to be part of our spiritual family, especially if we are drawn to that group over a long period of time; but this is not always the case. There is *no* outward sign that can tell us who we will feel this resonant energy with. It is a matter of inner knowing, and we have all had that experience of knowing at one time or another.

In a similar vein, the person who becomes our partner in life is often but not always part of our spiritual family. When this *is* the case, the partners support each other well in achieving their individual purposes and understand each other deeply. When this is not the case, as it is not in many marriages and long-term partner relationships, there can be much fighting, misunderstanding, and eventually separation. The partner of our present life may be a person who has been chosen on a soul level, not because she was to be supportive in an emotional sense, but because the greatest amount of learning could take place on a personality level in the presence of conflict and its resolution.

It is hard to imagine, Beloveds, why we do not choose to surround ourselves with dear friends and peaceful relationships throughout our lives, and why we cannot learn from the many souls with whom we share a deep spiritual bond. The answer is that we each have much to learn on the physical plane in order to become emotionally and spiritually whole, and this learning may require dealing with experiences and people who vibrationally we feel uncomfortable with. We are here to manifest our divinity, not just a part of our divinity, and so the qualities of courage, strength, determination, clarity, fearlessness, and trust, to name just a few, may require the presence of conflict or challenge of varying degrees in our lives in order to fully develop these qualities within our personality. When we can accept *all* situations that we find ourselves in as teachers, and can open to each of these, our learning will begin to take place on more and more subtle levels, and we will find our lives becoming more harmonious and peaceful as the remaining issues and challenges we deal with become internal, rather than external.

At this time, the challenge for each of us is to recognize the significance of each contact with another being that occurs during our ordinary day as a vital link in the chain of our learning. And it is to fully open to the possibilities of the moment, in even the most minor of interactions. There are loved ones from other times and places here today who have gifts for us that we cannot even perceive, if we do not have the awareness to treat each encounter as significant—and to act as if we are meeting a newly discovered member of our own family. By living in this way, we stop demeaning the beauty and value of our lives through our indifference to what we consider to be the less dramatic aspects of our ordinary days. We become challenged to see the everpresent beauty that fills even the most ordinary events with meaning, and presents us with new perspectives at every turn of the way.

When there are no more strangers for us in the world, when we see each other as brother and sister, then the heart can open fully to the day and to all events within it, for there is no one left to fear and no one left to judge. There is only love to be re-discovered.

When we can open our hearts to this quality of love, we become aware that it does not depend on time, or on how much we know about another person, or even on whether we could become friends with this person in our present reality. The love between souls depends solely on the openness that two people share in the moment—their mutual willingness to be totally present for each other at that moment in time.

Beloveds, when we can be totally present for another

being whom we do not know, we can learn to be totally present for ourselves, moment-to-moment; in this way do we learn to flow with the current of life, in harmony with all that is.

PAX

When nothing has to be repressed or denied, then the new can be exciting, scary, even uncomfortable, but we do not need to hold it off... The inner conviction grows that whatever happens, we will be capable of dealing with it...

Chapter 23

The Way of the Heart: The Opening

Beloveds, all love that we wish to extend to others must start with love for ourselves. For only in this beginning can we discover the compassion necessary to overlook all that stands in the way of love, as seen through the eyes of human perception. In opening the heart to ourselves, we begin by looking at those thoughts and feelings within us that have been rejected or considered unacceptable. We see these clearly, not with the eyes of criticism but with the eyes of compassion. In viewing ourselves in this way, we observe and trace the origin of all qualities that we would rather not have, and come to see that we could not have been any other way, given the circumstances we came from. We come to understand that these qualities were the very best we were capable of demonstrating in trying to cope with our lives. In such a category must we put those unwanted aspects of ourselves such as fear, impatience, envy, greed, selfishness, self-doubt, blame, resentment, withdrawal, superiority, and prejudice, to name just a few of our unwanted traits.

All of these, Beloveds, and more, have grown out of a need to protect ourselves from insurmountable difficulties as we perceived them, that we did not have the awareness to handle in a different way. In allowing these to come to the light of awareness now, we learn to forgive ourselves for *continuing* to lack the awareness of how to remove many of them, and we begin to see the need for a healing within ourselves that involves both an effort on our part to get clear, as well as the entrance of Grace into our lives.

What is critical in opening our hearts is both to *see ourselves clearly*, and to *ask for healing* from our higher Self—from our deepest self—that we may learn what the alternatives to these attitudes might be.

"I am a pure and blameless child of God; I forgive myself my (anger, etc.) and I ask for healing."*

Beloveds, this mantra or prayer for healing can be used by each of us at any time that an unwanted feeling-attitude emerges. It is to be used precisely at that moment when we feel incapable of transforming a negative emotion into a positive one. We breathe into the feeling-state and forgive ourselves right at that moment for having that particular feeling, and we recognize that that feeling has grown within us in order to protect our identity—to preserve us in a world of circumstances that we felt we had no power to change. These circumstances may have occurred in childhood or in a past life, or in several past lives—it makes no difference. The important thing is to open the heart to the feeling with complete forgiveness, and to be willing to experience the helplessness that was part of the original situation, when we did not know what else to do but to feel this particular way. In the presence of our openness and our request for healing, we invite a new light and a new perception into our hearts. We allow our higher Intelligence—our Spirit—to send messages to us and through us—messages that will help create a new awareness in our struggle to grow.

*From *A Course In Miracles* (Tiburon, California: Foundation for Inner Peace, 1985).

If I have yelled at the children today, or spoken critically to an employee, or gotten drunk again, or pushed my way ahead of someone else in line at the supermarket—if I have done any of these things *again* after telling myself that I would not—precisely at that moment of self-blame and experiencing defeat, I need to say:

"I am a pure and blameless child of God; I forgive myself my impatience and criticism and I ask for healing."

This thought, held in consciousness repeatedly, acts to detach us from the need to continue to behave in a similar fashion. For in forgiving ourselves and asking for healing, we also hold the unexpressed thought in mind: "I do not have to continue with this feeling; this is not me, for I am a blameless child of God. I will be helped to realize my true nature which is not *this behavior.*" It is a powerful moment for any of us when we can look at a behavior we have been struggling with, for example overeating, and instead of blaming ourselves for this as we have so many times in the past, say: this is just what I seem to need to be doing right now. How else can I look at this need? Let me open my mind to the other possibilities of satisfying what I am needing:

"I am a pure and blameless child of God; I forgive myself my overeating (or fear, or doubt) and I ask for healing."

It is not gone in an instant—the desire to overeat—and may not be gone for a very long time. But the decision to turn the matter over to higher Intelligence and to remain blameless does a great deal to detach our expectations from the prediction that this behavior will continue, and also does a great deal to reduce the very attitudes of self-blame that created the problem in the first place. There is no substitute for self-forgiveness, and all of us need to practice this all of the time.

When we have begun to live in a compassionate way toward ourselves, situations that are disappointing no longer affect us in the same way that they used to. For we grow accustomed to having an internal way of dealing with our disappointment, sadness, or dissatisfaction, and within the disappointing situation itself we no longer need to *blame ourselves* for having caused it, or to *blame others* either in order to feel better. We develop a capacity to contain and integrate the feelings of disappointment, and our natural capacity to digest these and to use them for our learning continually improves as we eliminate the need to erect defenses against them. This removes a great pressure in our lives. For when we don't *have to* have things be a certain way for us, when we know that crises that occur are really *crises of perception*, we can learn to see any situation through the eyes of compassion, rather than through the eyes of blame or fear.

By allowing our defensiveness to diminish, we become able to engage life and relationships in a more intimate way, for we no longer have to protect ourselves quite as much against unforeseen outcomes. Whether in a relationship with another person, or in our work, or in a new undertaking in any field, we can move forward toward an unknown outcome. Eventually, we can learn to allow ourselves to make a mistake and even to fail, knowing that our essential self remains at all times unharmed, and that even failure need not produce devestating self-criticism within us.

The ability to be on friendly terms with ourselves deepens as we come to realize that we are truly Souls, always struggling toward a higher and better understanding of how to respond to life. We have always been Souls, yet our experience of this truth needs to grow within our awareness, so that we can let go of the judgments of self and others that have weighed so heavily in our lives. When this happens, we become free just to enjoy our "is-ness," and can open in friendliness, in curiosity, and in appreciation to *how we are* at any particular moment in time.

Opening the heart to ourselves has many beneficial effects, not the least of which is ease in accepting new events in our lives, new situations, and changes within ourselves *When nothing has to be repressed or denied, then the new can be exciting, scary, even uncomfortable, but we do not need to hold it off.* We can allow ourselves to be scared, and still let the new into our perception and our life. This means that we become able to let go of the security of the familiar, and to let the breeze of change blow through our lives and our consciousness. We don't even have to know where we are going at any point in time, or who we are in any solid sense. The inner conviction grows that whatever happens, we will be capable of dealing with it on inner levels.

In this way we can open to deeper places within ourselves that have been sealed off for years, perhaps for lifetimes. We can experiment with situations that we may not have dared to try out while we needed to ward off "failure." We can become new to ourselves, day by day and year by year, allowing our openness to create whatever changes in perception occur naturally within us. This openness to change allows the doors of perception to open on many levels. Not only can we afford to see ourselves in a truer light when our vision doesn't need to be denied or protected, but we allow the *deeper knowing of the real* to become more conscious within us, whether that be a deeper knowing of the real within another person, or a deeper knowing of the real within the cosmos. Our openness to ourselves opens us to all beings and to all of life.

This much can be said regarding the fear of change and the fear of opening—that the more we risk seeing and hearing the true voice within us, even when that voice is not pleasant, the more we hear the true voice within life, as inner truth becomes matched by the perception of outer truth more and more. Change itself does not seem as frightening then, when it is supported by our inner truth, as well as by circumstances around us which are seen to comprise one seamless fabric—one whole.

In the face of fear of what we shall find within us, we need only to breathe deeply, to create space around the uncomfortable feeling which simply allows it to *be* within our awareness. In the process of giving it space, and room within our consciousness, we discover that fear itself (or anger or sadness) is nothing to be afraid of. They are just feelings—and they lead to other feelings and other states of awareness as we open to them.

Beloveds, the new integration that is possible as we open compassionately to our inner truth brings us to a heightened state of appreciation of ourselves as unique creatures within a world filled with uniqueness and interest. As we attain self-mastery by permitting the wholeness of the self within, we discover more and more that our inner wholeness is matched by outer wholeness everywhere we look, and that there is no part of the puzzle that is missing in our perception of the real.

Let us therefore take the time in kindness and appreciation of ourselves, to set before our inner eyes those parts of ourselves that we would, in times past, have chosen to get rid of. Let us welcome these parts into our awareness as guests and teachers and ask each one what it has to teach us. With this receptivity toward the total self, we can then find the freedom to grow more quickly as we wish to. For we have opened the doors of our heart to let the sunlight in, and all that we now are can become one with all that we wish to be.

PAX

Can we, who seek love, find the love in our hearts that will outflow even where there is no need being expressed, and especially no need for our love? Can we feel our desire to love so strongly that we allow it to radiate out and bless others before they ask for our blessing, knowing that this is what each heart desires, even when it is not saying so out loud?

Chapter 24

The Way of the Heart: Loving

Beloveds, the path that love takes as it becomes more and more pure in its expression is one that is sometimes seen within the parent-child relationship as a newborn is welcomed into the world. At this time in the experience of loving, ideally there are no conditions or demands placed upon the infant. That being is simply welcomed into one's heart as he or she is, without preconception, without understanding of an intellectual kind, without any desire except to cherish and nurture that new life—to give to it those essential ingredients that are necessary for both its survival and its growth. At this time, the newborn returns to the parents only the gift of its existence, the gift of its being present; it does not have any other gifts to trade other than the statement: I Am. And this is enough. For with this statement comes the experience of belonging on the part of the parent, and of participation in that tiny being's life. It is much more than a matter of being needed in a practical, concrete sense, although that too is part of the feeling of love; it is a sense of union, of belongingness, of participation in the deepest meaning of each others' lives that is at the foundation of the bond between parent and child.

This, dear ones, is a model for love in all forms, not only

that which occurs within the parent-child context. It is love as God intended us to love one another: unconditional, asking to receive only the "I Am" statement of the beloved; asking to nurture and care for the essential being of that other; seeking to join, to belong, to participate in the shared meaning of that other being's life which is intertwined with one's own. This essential quality of love can be felt toward friends, toward family, toward lovers or mates, toward animals, toward nature, and toward all beings. It is a feeling of the soul which seeks to nurture and create life at whatever level it engages with it. At this level, love reflects the creative impulse of the Universe—the force of evolution—forever bringing the new out of the old. All life grows and thrives based on this universal principle of loving.

Now it is clear that within our present society this is not the way that we have been taught to love. From an early age we have been taught that love is conditional—that we must be good or we will be disapproved of; that there are certain behaviors that we can enact that will take love away from us. This is the typical pattern of early learning and conditioning, and it is continually reinforced by countless social, sexual, and occupational situations later on. We are *not* loved for who we are; we are loved for what we do. And this becomes drilled into us over and over again as we move through adulthood, until we give up all hope of ever finding the other again in that sense of mysterious and mystical participation that was part of our memory of infancy, and even further back, of life before birth on the planes of Spirit.

It does no good, dear ones, to helplessly declaim the fact that society conveys these attitudes toward all of her children, the young and the old alike—that it restricts and inhibits us from becoming who we are. What must happen is a revolution in thinking and feeling within each of us individually. We must resolve to form a new society of beloveds, consisting of each and every person who wants to be free of the restrictions on his natural expression, and who wants to be loved for himself.

All of us long for the freedom to be. Those who seek it consciously and deliberately have the vision to offer to others what they wish to receive themselves: love that does not ask except to give, to nurture, and to provide the conditions in which another can thrive—love that recognizes belongingness with another based on nothing other than the statement: I Am; love that recognizes the joining between ourselves and another—the knowing that we have a common purpose and share a common meaning. This love is limitless, and can be offered to those who are near to us, and to those whom we don't even know. The sense of belonging will differ in *intensity* with those with whom we live and have an ongoing relationship, but the *quality* of loving need not differ. Love is love and can be offered to all.

Beloveds, can we find within our hearts a place of courage to begin to share our love in this way? To recognize our kinship and belonging with others even though they may not recognize theirs with us? This is the challenge, beloveds, for those whom we seek to love may not acknowledge us in the way that an infant acknowledges the nursing breast or the comforting parent. That infant is responding partly out of the instinctual survival mechanisms that have been built into his physical being, and partly out of the pressing sense of need every infant feels. This need reinforces the parent's sense of belonging and of participation with the child.

Can we, who seek love, find the love in our hearts that will flow outwardly even where there is no need being expressed, and especially no need for our love? Can we feel our desire to love so strongly that we allow it to radiate out and bless others before they ask for our blessing, knowing that this is what each heart desires, even when it is not saying so out loud?

Let us look into our own hearts, beloveds, to see if this is possible.

What kind of world would we wish to live in if we could—a world filled with strangers and a few friends, with many being afraid or embarrassed to look each other in the eye, or a world in which the word "stranger" had disappeared, and each person whom we met, even casually on the street, had the potential to form a deep and lasting heart connection with us? Which would we choose: to live in a world where only a few people mattered to us and our individual lives affected only a few others, or to live in a world where many others mattered to us and our actions and thoughts could improve the welfare and lives of countless others?

This is the choice beloveds, and it is a choice that we each must make in sincerity from the deepest part of our hearts. We may not feel ready for this kind of love; it may feel like too much of a responsibility for us. Yet the world is in need of each and every one of us taking responsibility for breaking down the barriers that separate us, and if we each do not choose to do it, who will? For *we* are society, and each one of us individually determines the length of time that barriers between individuals, between classes, between races, and between nations shall remain. We each have the power to decide what we can do to love more in our immediate life-situations at this very moment.

What is important to remember is that there is no danger in opening our hearts in this way if our intention is sincere, and if we are asking only to give life and love to nurture the life in others, not covertly asking that we receive something in return. The newborn infant does not smile immediately after it is born, in fact does not even recognize faces for a while. And during this period, the parent is not really known as a parent, and the determination to love unconditionally maintains itself without much reinforcement from the infant's response. This is possible since emotional contact and a feeling of belonging exist from the beginning.

In our adult lives too, emotional contact and a sense of belonging must be felt first—we cannot sincerely bring love forth when there is no perceived connection, for the response of love comes only in those situations where we are *capable* of seeing or sensing the *inner being* of another whom we wish to help and bless. So let us start with just those situations in which we feel especially close to someone, or especially protective or sympathetic. When we already recognize the inner beauty or inner pain within another, we have made the necessary contact and can begin to see a vision of their soul. Let us start wherever we are, with whomever we cherish, to whatever degree. We can start by ridding our minds of those conditions which involve a trade- off of the kind: "I will love you if you will do for me, and if not, I won't love you." Wherever we are making our love reactive or responsive to what someone else is doing to us, we are diminishing our capacity to love. At these times, we need to say inwardly to ourselves: "I will love you even if you are *not* doing for me what I wish you to do."

Dear ones, loving does not mean accepting every action that another does without judgment. It does not mean allowing ourselves to be hurt either physically or emotionally; it does not mean putting ourselves in false situations in the name of love. Loving means opening in the moment to whatever degree is possible, to *see* the inner being of another—and to bless it, to wish it well, to hope for its growth and nourishment, and to offer to that *inner being* whatever help can be offered.

There are times when we meet people in ordinary life who seem very disconnected from their inner being and it feels difficult to love these people. This is understandable.

It takes practice and the willingness to reach out past rejection, indifference, withdrawal, and fear, to let our own love find that light within another—a light which they themselves may be totally unaware of. This can be done, but it can only be done by us when we have become stronger in *self-love*, so that rejection and indifference no longer deter us from expressing our true nature.

In the present, let us start with those around us who can offer us a little feedback, so that we will know that our efforts to love unconditionally are being recognized. It is not wrong to prefer feedback and appreciation, for we have not relinquished our own desire to *be loved* which is part of our humanness. So we can start with those situations where we have been stingy with our love—afraid of being embarrassed, afraid of being rejected, or of being seen as strange. Let us allow in our minds that we will be acting unconventionally from society's standpoint, to express love openly and often, for that is not the nature of the world we live in. But it is the nature of the world we *wish* to live in, and we need to begin to create it *now*.

Embarrassment is a small price to pay for the ability to help an infant thrive, to bring a smile to someone's face, or to help another change her ideas about what is permissible for her to express. When we open ourselves to being loving, risking acting in unconventional ways, we create a permission for others to also act in similar ways, and even if they do not respond to us with greater openness *at that moment*, we are joining them on an inner level within their hearts, in the place within that wishes for the same kind of sharing that we wish for. In that deep place within we share with them our own sense of belonging and of participation in their lives.

Beloveds, we have stood apart from our true capacity to love out of fear and disillusionment, and out of the desire to spare ourselves the hurt of rejection. These are concepts that we hold that we can let go of now, in the Light of our

Soul which reveals to us our true nature. In this Light, we can ask for courage that as we embark upon a path of freedom to be ourselves, as we open ourselves emotionally to the greatness of the love within us—that we may find the means to express this truth of our being, and to help others to open as well. Together, through love, may we learn to perpetually bless each other's growth.

PAX

Dear ones, the angels are always with each of us, sending their rays of love and hope to us at every moment. When we call to them and ask for their help and guidance, we create a doorway between worlds that invites them to become even more present within our energy fields and within our lives.

Chapter 25

The Angelic Kingdom

B the kingdom of the angels has always existed in litera-
ture and lore and in the heart of prayer within each of
us. The angelic is the pure, the good, and the true that we
aspire to, and our souls sing with joy when we meet angelic
radiance on the human plane.

The angels, Beloveds, are real. And they embody these
ideals, because they are the repositors and protectors of all
of mankind's ideals and the creators of form for their expression on the plane of manifestation. One of their most
exalted tasks is to bequeath to those who seek their purity
the Divine inspiration to create works of artistic majesty
and greatness which reflect God's glory. Such are the
works of a Beethoven or Mozart. Such are the paintings of
Da Vinci and Botticelli, of Raphael and Fra Angelico.
These paintings were inspired by the angelic realm, and
existed within this realm as pure idea waiting for form.

The angels are the builders of form within the
Universe—form that will embody an ideal image. Thus,
they are entrusted with that part of the Divine plan that
has to do with bringing into manifestation the next step in
the evolution of life collectively, and of life individually. In
the process of conceiving and giving birth to a child, for
example, the angels hold the pattern of energy for the

child that will be, as one might hold a suit of clothes that one is about to try on. They hold the pattern in their minds, you might say, and when the time for materialization occurs, they take this pattern of energy or thought, and transform it by adding to it increasing layers of denser energy, until the pattern becomes solidified into physical form on the cellular level within the fertilized egg. Each cell contains the pattern of the whole, and the pattern that will emerge of the human child is already present in the first cell of conception.

The process of angelic creation works from the greatest to the most microscopic level of form-building. The angels are guardians of creation for each of us at all times in our lives, but especially when we ask for their presence to be with us. When we seek to express an ideal of beauty, truth, love, harmony, unity—or any ideal that we aspire to, this aspiration reaches up into the heavens and draws the angelic to us.

Beloveds, each life-form, including those of plants and animals, is watched over by angelic beings whose task it is to regulate and maintain the consistency of conditions which nurture that form and bring it into fuller growth. This process may be made clearer as we watch a plant growing in the sunlight. Each plant has a little angel or deva watching over it which maintains its ideal essence. The deva, on an energy level, supervises the process of integration of the elements that nourish the plant from without such as sun, rain, air, earth, as well as the process by which an individual plant takes in and uses these elements. The angels do this not through some kind of external "authority," but through the transforming and transmitting functions of their own energy bodies.

Angels and devas are guardians and supervisors of the material world and their help to us is constant. For that help is their purpose for being and brings them joy and fulfillment. When we feel alone and unprotected in life situations, Beloveds, it is not because we are so in fact. Our sense of lack creates what might be considered to be an astral cloud around us, a fog in our auric field, that fills our aura with thoughts of sadness, depression, or fear, and does not allow us to take in the angelic radiance existing within our own atmosphere. It would be as if we were walking outside on a beautiful day, but because of our mood could not notice that it was sunny or warm, or that the air smelled fresh. Many of us, because of our emotional state, seal ourselves off from noticing the angelic forces around us which are felt as light, as upliftment, as a surge of joy or happiness within the heart.

Dear ones, the angels are always with each of us, sending their rays of love and hope to us at every moment. When we call to them and ask for their help and guidance, we create a doorway between worlds that invites them to become even more present within our energy fields and within our lives. Ask then for their help in all that you do Beloveds, and you will begin to feel the lightness of certain success in your hearts, as you realize that all help is being given to you to accomplish your aims.

On a higher level within the angelic kingdom are the angels that preside over larger areas of manifestation, and that hold the ideals for an entire area of the Earth. These angels are not quite as exalted in responsibility or in consciousness as the Archangels, but they are more so than the angels, spirits, and devas that watch over individual development. These are the angels of the forests, the mountains, and the oceans. Great angelic beings ensoul whole areas of the world. A mountain has its own angelic spirit that is identified with and holds the essential pattern or ideal for the essence of that mountain. The same is true of a lake or a forest. A large physical body or geographical area has an identity in much the same way that we as individuals have identities, and its persona, or feeling-tone, can be felt by all who visit it. For example, the particular quality of a lake set in the mountains has color, depth, setting, relationship to wind, temperature, etc., and each of these physical elements affects the emotional reaction that individuals have to being in its presence. On the soul level, the Spirit of that lake holds the pattern for its beauty and the quality of feeling it is meant to express within nature. Often, the artist's highly attuned eye can capture the Spirit within the natural form, while others who are less sensitive merely see the physical.

There is nothing on Earth in physical form, Beloveds, that does not have an ensouling Spirit or angel holding its pattern, and helping it to maintain its ideal essence. Forests have presiding angels, as do oceans, and land masses. Nations in particular have ensouling angels who hold the form of the essential quality of the nation, and who vibrationally (one could almost say atmospherically), communicate this pattern or essence to all persons connected with the nation as a group. In this way, the common ideal of what that nation is striving for and what it represents, is held within the collective mind or culture, and also within the individual minds of those affected by that culture.

Angelic vibrations surround the Earth with their love and good will at all times, and they have done much at times of chaos and destruction upon the Earth to counteract the prevailing negativity and to preserve the balance of light over darkness. This is done through consciousness, rather than through actual "work" in the angelic realms; for the angels hold in their consciousness the perfect pattern for the Earth's evolution and development. Even at times when the Earth seems to be stalled in this development or on a destructive course, angelic consciousness maintains the flow toward the principles of Light.

More powerful, more responsible, and more exalted in

their consciouness are the Archangels, the greatest of whom have become known to mankind through the writings and paintings of visionaries, mystics, and contemplatives who at times have made contact with them. The Archangels are the right hand of God in the scheme of manifesting the Universe. They are the authors and supervisors of whole realms of creation. Stars, solar systems, planets, entire races of people, and entire civilizations are presided over by the greatest of the Archangels. These Blessed Ones watch over the development of humanity as a whole and at different historical periods, one or another of them take responsibility for fostering that period's development into the expression of a phase-specific goal. This occurs by influencing the thought patterns of the culture as a whole, and of specific individuals within that culture whose ideas will have widespread influence.

Vast numbers of people within a given historical period are influenced by a few key ideas expressed powerfully by a limited number of voices at first. These ideas are then taken up by a larger number of voices and over time become part of the mainstream cultural thought pattern. By inspiring the leaders, artists, scientists, and philosphers of an age, the Archangels help to disseminate the phase-specific ideals. As time passes, they help to bring each age into fullness and to set the stage for the next epoch that will express within the historical drama.

In this way, the Earth today is being influenced by the angels and Archangels. In our present period of transformation and change, new ideas are springing forth everywhere regarding planetary consciousness and responsibility to the Earth and to one another. These ideas, just twenty-five years ago, were part of the awareness of only a few individuals. Gradually, throughout these last three decades, ideals for a whole new way of living have become part of a new culture calling itself the New Age. And the angels and Archangels have been instrumental in instilling life and inspiration into the ideals themselves, and into the people who express them. In this way does history transform itself as each step leads to the next in the course of human evolution.

Throughout all of their work in creating and maintaining life, the angels and Archangels are motivated by the highest and purest kind of love that we can conceive of. They exist within this state of love at all times, a love which comes from the constant awareness of the oneness of all life, and the perception of themselves as brothers and sisters, mothers and fathers to all beings.

It is this infinite love which allows them to maintain the ideal pattern for all beings, for they are never persuaded that any expression that deviates from the ideal pattern— whether of an individual, a group, or a nation—is more than temporary, or that it interferes with the ultimate growth into wholeness of that being. The angels see with perpetual delight the emerging wholeness of each and every one of us; they see us moving into the fulfillment of our Divine pattern and so they can be quite gay and cheerful, even in the midst of what from a human level might be considered suffering or evil.

For Beloveds, the angelic realm knows that all that we consider to be "evil" is only temporary, and holds no ultimate power over the forces of Love and Truth. Evil is only given life by the consciousness that believes in it, and when all beings no longer find evil within themselves, but instead find only God, evil will not be able to exist as a reality any more for there will be no thought within or without to feed it.

Beloveds, the angelic realm blesses us continually with its desire to bestow upon us the gifts of grace, truth, and joy. We can invite the angels into our lives daily, and especially at times of need, through the purity of our intention to reach for the highest within ourselves. When we do so, we find ourselves guided toward the Light within that is eternally part of God's vision of us and of the angelic vision of us as well.

Know that we are at all times held and blessed by their love.

PAX

PART IV: *Transformation*

Do not fear that you will lose your identity in this process of surrender, for each of you is a soul, and no soul that has been created can ever lose its essential individuality. It is only to become brighter and more aware of oneself that the process of surrender is chosen, that the One may become many and the many become One.

Chapter 26

The Message of Mary

"I am the handmaiden of the lord; let it be unto me according to Thy word."

*I who stand before you in an age of deceit and despair hold a lamp in my hand whose flame is trust in the unborn future; for I **am** the unborn future that exists within all of you, the faith yet stirring in the womb of doubt and uncertainty. Keeping the flame of love for all hearts that yearn to love, and holding this flame near to God's breath, so that that Divine breath may ever warm the slightest movement to love that issues forth from His children.*

*I am the light of the pure in speech, in thought, and in deed, and he who would seek the golden jewel of perfection within himself shall follow the way of purity, for perfection is linked to purity as an end is to a beginning. The light of the sacred that seeks a dwelling place within the heart of each child of God is nurtured by the purest of wishes that light may be victorious over darkness, within and without. There is no other truth than this: that victory **shall** inevitably come to the forces of Light and Love, for all else is not of Spirit and must perish. Yet within the reaches of time can one call to the flame of the indwelling Spirit, and hasten* *the day when sorrow shall leave and joy find its way here, by perfecting that sweet surrender of mind and body to Spirit and allowing the body to become the temple of the Lord.*

I am the light of the Divine rooted in matter—the substance of all things—of the very particles which spin within the atom. I am the connecting force holding the world of the physical in place, and liberating it at its proper time from the confines of material identification. I, the Divine Mother, bring travellers home through the physical plane, home to the love of their spiritual being. I am rest for the weary, healing for the sick, and hope for the despairing. I am the light of the Divine.

There can be no hope for humanity as a whole or for individuals in particular, when hope is bested by cynicism and a limited view of the particular events currently taking place on the world stage—as if the Divine light were not always present. See through and beyond these events in your lives, collectively and individually, to the perfection that is being created even now within the seedbed of ferment and dissatisfaction. Hope is necessary to bring in the future, and hope can only be nurtured within the confines of darkness and uncertainty, else it would not be hope. Trust is the same, requiring a period of waiting in darkness in order to grow into its full light and measure. These are the Divine qualiies that humanity is beginning to embody even now, that will flourish and bloom as the New Age comes into its full embodiment here on the Earth plane.

*Seek now the Light within your hearts, and when you find it, ask that you be guided and aided to surrender your little Light, that it may become an even brighter flame as it is joined with the greater Light of the Universe. **Do not fear that you will lose your identity in this process of surrender, for each of you is a soul, and no soul that has been created can ever lose its essential individuality. It is only to become***

brighter and more aware of oneself that the process of surrender is chosen, that the One may become many, and the many become One. *This paradox of identity and individuality cannot be comprehended by those who do not yet realize the full glory that comes to those who are poor in personal glory, and who achieve through that the knowledge of their magnificence as part of the God Who lives within all.*

Therefore seek not to sustain yourself by the standards of an outward success which is temporary, and only serves to perpetuate the illusion of the ego that much longer. Desire to find the inner truth of your Spirit, which seeks to glorify God, the One Being within each heart worthy of all glory. This does not mean rejecting success or attainment when it comes to you on the material plane, for that too is simply an outer manifestation of the indwelling Spirit. But rather know that all comes from God and that all is a gift from the Divine, rather than a possession.

There is but one possession for the children of God, and that is their Spirit which exists forever. All else is an illusion. Therefore seek to release all that the heart clings to that feels necessary, other than the will of Spirit, for only this shall remain after all else disappears. See that the physical world is ruled by the law of rhythm and of change and that nothing here today shall remain very long on this plane. That is the nature of the material. Therefore have faith in holding only to the Light of the flame within the heart— that Light which creates hope anew each morning and each moment, even in the midst of uncertainty and doubt. Hold to that Light and let it guide you through all periods of indecision and of despair.

For this Light is your beacon and shall never leave you, as is the flame I hold for all of humanity. This flame exists to guide you in your search for the purity and courage that are so necessary at this present time—in this present trans-

formation of planetary consciousness. Know that I am with you and that God is with you, and that each one will be guided to that particular destiny that is your own soul's choosing, to manifest that which you are most capable of expressing as a beautiful and precious child of God.

PAX

Dear ones, the path of the sword, also called the "path of initation," does not follow one particular spiritual practice, philosophy, or school of thought. . . it is the last stage on the path toward higher consciousness, and each being who has chosen a particular teacher, spiritual practice, or context for learning within a given lifetime will one day bow only before the inner Teacher—the only true Guide on this path.

Chapter 27

The Path of the Sword

Beloveds, there are three rewards for one who pursues the path of the sword with courage, faith, and detachment, and these are found at its end. They are Completion, Mastery, and Enlightenment. The first brings to the self an awareness of the fulfillment of love; the second brings to the self an awareness of the totality of freedom; the third brings to the self an awareness of the Truth of unity with all that is.

The path of the sword is the path of struggle, of trial, and of progress in discriminating that which is of greater truth from that which is of lesser truth so that falseness can be eliminated from our life. it is also the path of purification upon which we uproot the foundations of desire within ourselves, purifying our motives until only the desire to express our indwelling divinity remains.

Only the committed and the dedicated can maintain the strength needed to traverse this path consistently, for the way is steep and hard to travel. Yet here are the greatest rewards for the seeker, for he or she will, in significantly less time than it takes to progress through the ordinary cycle of life and learning, meet the challenges of karma head on and thus greatly reduce the time taken to achieve the triune goals of Completion, Mastery, and Enlightenment.

These goals, Beloveds, lie ahead for *all* beings in time, whether the progress toward them be slow or quick. The choice of approach belongs to each of us and it is made on a soul level and on a personal level for each lifetime. Over time, generally toward the end of a reincarnational cycle, the soul begins to see the end of its efforts on the Earth plane in sight, and therefore may choose to speed up the process of growth in consciousness by appropriating to itself greater challenges and difficulties in the lifetimes that remain. In these later lifetimes then, the awakening human will begin to hear the call of the higher Self and to slip out of the outworn garments of the personal self, leaving them behind forever.

Dear ones, the path of the sword, also called the "path of initiation," does not follow one particular spiritual practice, philosophy, or school of thought. Rather it is the way that all schools and philosophies point to, for it is the last stage on the path toward higher consciousness, and each being who has chosen a particular teacher, spiritual practice, or context for learning within any given lifetime, will one day bow only before the inner Teacher—the only true Guide on this path.

Championing the cause of all who strive toward attainment on the path is the Archangel Michael who, holding the flaming sword of Truth, Power, and Love, assists all who would become one with truth to rid the lower self of all that holds it back in its efforts to purify. Archangel Michael holds the sword of discrimination in his right hand. In his left, he holds the scales of justice which weigh the actions and words of each being in terms of the Light and Love they carry. In helping those on the path, he offers his sword for our own use, and his scales that we may more quickly judge what remains within us that needs to be released.

Along with Michael as helper and wayshower is Mary, the mother of Jesus— symbol of the purity accompanying travellers on this path. Mary's emblem is the "mystic rose"—the rose of purity—which assists in the purification of those who would claim the vision of the Highest for their own. This rose, symbolically mounted on the sword, uses the weapon of discrimination and truth to help each one to open more and more to the purity of Spirit.

The mystic rose has been worn by others who stand out in history, yet among them the spirit of Mary illumines the way for us by totally embodying that purity of essence that the rose stands for, and by transmitting to the consciousness of those who seek it a standard with which each can compare her own consciousness. For it is the desire for purity of Spirit and purity in one's life, that brings the rose into bloom within our awareness, signalling our willingness to experience the death of the lower self and of the personal desire nature. The rose and the sword, dear ones, are aspects of awareness that we bring to ourselves through our deepening commitment to walk upon the spiritual path.

Beloveds, this deepening commitment of the self is the single most important factor that opens the path of initiation to those who choose it. Entrance upon this path has no other criteria than that of spiritual dedication, and only this enables the seeker to maintain sufficient faith, courage, and detachment to walk along its way. One day, each of us will traverse this path, for the path of the sword, the path of initiation, defines a level of advancement spiritually, and a stage in the evolution of our soul on its journey home. At this stage a transition occurs for us between consciously living our life as a human being embedded in matter, and consciously living our life as a Divine being embedded in Spirit.

The symbol for this path and for this stage of evolution is the six- pointed star, containing two equilateral triangles, one facing upward and the other down. The up-ward facing triangle represents the human being struggling to realize his Divine consciousness; the downward point-ing triangle is the Divine Spirit or higher Self, struggling to unite with the being within physical form. The marriage of these two aspects of oneself—the human and the Divine, has often been referred to as the "mystic marriage," and awareness at this level creates a shift in consciousness which forever changes the individual personality and the individual life. For it brings to all actions and all percep-tions on the physical plane a transcendent meaning and beauty which can only be seen from the plane of the Soul.

There is a stage of preparation needed before becoming ready for the marriage of the material and the spiritual within us. During this preparation period, the progressive refinement of our sensitivity to spiritual reality is needed. For there would be no point in attempting to struggle with the many challenges and hardships on the way of initiation if we did not already have the sword of Truth in hand to some degree, and if we were not already convinced beyond question of the existence of spiritual reality in general, and for ourselves in particular.

Therefore, before the entrance to the path *is recognized*, and during the stage of preparation, we begin to recognize within ourselves the voice of our Soul, calling us to a higher standard of thought and action than the everyday world generally perceives as valid. Response to this inner voice readies us for the journey that follows—a journey which begins when we are determined to consciously take the final steps necessary to join our humanity with our divinity, through the deliberate elimination of all that stands in the way. When this point is reached there devel-ops on its own a longing in us for the ideals of Love, Unity, and Freedom—a longing which cannot any longer be sup-pressed.

The desire for Love is felt as a call to wholeness—a

desire to experience and to live as a *whole self*. All relationships and all situations which require us to limit the self or to falsify it are let go of in pursuit of the sensed ideal of wholeness with ourselves in Love.

The desire for Mastery is felt as a call to understand the power of thought to influence our lives, and the beginning of a need to regulate thought so that it contains only that which is felt to lead to God.

The desire for Englightenment is felt as a yearning to end the state of separation that divides us from life around us, and as a loneliness that can only be satisfied by coming Home to spiritual being.

The experience of these purified desires for Completion, Mastery, and Englightenment, leads inevitably to the end of the journey, Beloveds, and fulfillment awaits each of us at this end:

- We discover that perfection of love in which we are completely seen, completely loved, and completely aware of our own lovingness. This is the first attainment.

- We become free to create our lives and limitless in the choices we can make. This is the goal of Mastery, and it leaves the individual who has become one with Spirit supremely powerful in relation to the material world. This is the second attainment.

- We become aware of our unity with all beings and with all of life, and lose the sense of separation from all others that we have lived with. This is the goal of Truth and Unity, and it is the third attainment.

Beloveds, at the end of our journey is the certain fulfillment of these three goals. It is up to each of us to hear how they call to us even now, and to allow the voice of Spirit to speak to us from the deepest place within our hearts.

TEACHING THE HEART TO SING

When we are ready to respond to this call with a whole heart, the path of the sword will open before us, and we will each begin the final stage of our journey Home.

May Love that awaits us aid us on our way.

PAX

Doubt is a function of our forgetting that
all of reality is a creation of the mind,
brought into being out of the energy of con-
sciousness at different levels of
awareness . . .

Chapter 28

Standing Firm

Beloveds, doubt and the perception of duality are inseparable in our lives. For when we feel ourselves to be powerless to affect a particular outcome that we desire, it is because we are seeing a separation between our *will-power* or our *creative life energy* and external events. In reality, there is *no* separation between these two, other than that created by our thought process. The attitude of powerlessness which doubt initiates creates an inner image of separation between the outer and the inner which remains false, while we believe it to be true.

Beloveds, when doubt comes into our hearts, moving us to give in or give up, we can gain strength from the image of the mountain which, standing firm, displays that essential quality of stolidness and implacability that can also be ours. To learn to stand firm in the face of doubt, we must first fully realize that doubt is a *learned* response, not a necessary one. When a young child falls down and gets hurt in the process of learning to walk, it does not doubt that it will eventually master walking; it does not give up because it falls down time after time. In a similar fashion, our belief in our inherent capacity to achieve the goals we set for ourselves can get us where we wish in much the same fashion as a child learns to walk. We did not lose this capacity, dear ones; we have just *forgotten* that we were once confident that anything we wished for we could manifest.

Doubt is a function of our forgetting that all of reality is a **creation of the mind,** *brought into being out of the energy of consciousness at different levels of awareness*—out of the unconscious, conscious, and superconscious minds—and manifesting in external energy patterns of different degrees of solidity. All that we consider to be reality is continually influenced by the mental process that takes place within each of us individually and within all of us collectively. *All* that we consider to be negative in our experience is a function of what we ourselves have thought, and have brought into being at some time in the past. It is necessary to remember this when life does not present us with what we hoped for, and when we begin to question the order and benevolence of the Universe.

When external events seem the most unpredictable and unacceptable to us, it is because our ongoing belief in the *duality* of the inner and outer worlds is continuing to operate to maintain the illusion of separation. This way of thinking must be unlearned if we are to begin to create our lives consciously, with attention to what is needed for each of us personally and for the planet as a whole.

We have been given the gift of free-will as Divine children of the Creator. When we realize the meaning of this and begin to *activate our will,* we set in motion a stream of energy that remains perpetually in operation—just like a car engine that has been left running. Although we may not be consciously thinking of a particular goal, our unconscious mind, once convinced that we really mean business about desiring a particular thing, goes to work to manifest this in the Universe. We are creatures of will, and at every moment we are pulling some event, or person, or experience into existence through the force of the energy we send out.

Doubt occurs when what we perceive to be our *will* and what we perceive to be *external reality* are felt to be in conflict. It is especially at this time that we must learn to stand firm in our *intentionality*.

We must continue to send our intentions out into the Universe, absolutely undismayed by any evidence that seems to contradict them. For our will has been given to us by God, that we may learn to use it to create life in infinite variety and according to our liking. At this point in our development, we are just waking up to the possibility that this might be true—that our thoughts about reality actually have a significant effect on what we experience.

When an apparent contradiction occurs between what is outside us and what is inside us and we question our power to change the external, let us remember that what already exists has been created by our past thoughts, generated in this lifetime or in past lives. These thoughts remain within our auras long after our conscious minds have stopped thinking them. They continue to influence our present reality until we consciously reclaim them and release them.

We being to change the present, beloveds, not by focusing on the past but by focusing on the *future* in terms of what we wish to create in our lives. Let us see the future as emerging out of the *now*, and the present as if it were a passing show, giving way to the next scene in the movie of our life. In looking at the present in this way, we can hold the idea in our minds that the movie is being created by *us* and that at each moment we are revising the script for what will be in the next frame and the next reel.

There is nothing in the movie of our lives that cannot be changed if we choose to recognize the God within us, and become conscious of our parts as writers and directors of the movie itself.

In practice, this means that when doubt assails us, tempting us to believe that we will be unsuccessful in manifesting what we desire, we redouble our intention to *will* what we wish into existence. Believing that we have the capacity to do so overcomes fifty percent of doubt. The other fifty percent is overcome by our *standing firm in our intentionality* on both conscious and unconscious levels, and continuing to be convinced that what we desire will come to us.

This is not a fanciful idea dreamed up by writers of folk and fairy tales in pleasanter times. The basis of this 'myth' is the presentiment of a truth once known but forgotten. In our present time, the truth of our creative power is being recovered as our personalities begin to integrate more fully around our mental process, and we become willing to experience the contents of our conscious and unconscious minds with greater clarity and acceptance. This is a major step forward in our personal and collective transformation.

Before this time of personality integration at the mental level, when emotional needs dominated and the unconscious ruled our lives because it *remained unconscious*, it would not have been possible for us to activate our will in the sense that we now can. For unknown to us, the unconscious mind would have sent out contradictory thought patterns to what the conscious mind dictated.

At a stage in life when an individual's thoughts are tied up with emotional need, thoughts themselves have limited power to affect change, especially external change. This is so not only because of the frequent conflict between the conscious and unconscious impulse, but just as importantly because thoughts burdened by emotional need tend to *manifest repetitive external situations*, based on desires from the past. The logic of the emotions tells us that if an important emotional situation in our lives did not work out in the past and left us feeling badly about ourselves, if we repeat it over and over again eventually we will be able to make it come out better. This is especially true of situations that occurred in childhood that are repeated endlessly throughout adulthood so that a healing of our self-perception can take place. It is also why many people find partners who are similar to their parents, so that early life situations can be recreated with a different outcome.

For the most part, this drive toward mastery of past wounds occurs on an unconscious level, and makes us vulnerable to a thought pattern that at best is limiting, and at worst is experienced as repeatedly painful. Emotional need creates pressure on the creative potential of the mind, transforming the mind into a vehicle for the satisfaction of that need. Only when the mind is relatively free on both conscious and unconscious levels, can it seek to creatively bring something new into our lives, something desirable that has not existed before. When this is the case, in a manner both easy and natural, the mind simply begins to focus clearly and repetitively on that which is desired, and the will sends out the thought into the Universe:

"Because I want it to happen, it *will* happen."

People who believe this strongly are considered to be strong-willed and many of them have been leaders throughout history. Having a strong will does not necessarily mean putting into action principles or practices that are beneficial for others; rather, it means having a sense of power, of destiny, and of the ability to conquer all obstacles that stand in the way of the fulfillment of our goals. People who are considered to have "weak wills" still feel victimized by their personal, social, racial, or cultural history, and have not yet developed the sense of personal power which intuitively understands the relationship between thought and external events.

Beloveds, the seeds of change are now in the air for each of us individually and for humanity as a whole. Many of us are ready to make that leap into creative expression and control over our own lives through mastery of the thought process. Many of us are being guided in doing this not only by our conscious desires, but by the messages of our higher Self. The higher Self, speaking through the "superconscious mind," transmits information to us about what is beneficial or desirable for us as souls, rather than what is beneficial for us as personalities.

There is nothing that can stop one who chooses to take control of his life in this way except inner doubt—doubt which understandably grows when time elapses between the awareness of willing a certain outcome and intending to create a particular form, and the outer manifestation of our intentionality. When outer events, for long periods of time do not reflect the successful materialization of our wishes into form and the transformation of thought-energy into matter, we tend to become discouraged and feel defeated by time itself. As if time were an enemy—a barrier between ourselves and the fulfillment of what we desire. Time, dear ones, can always be counted on to be a friend. It is simply the *medium* in which energy becomes matter. We might think of it as putting a bath oil bead into a warm bathtub. The bead will eventually dissolve, spreading its fragrant essence throughout the water. Yet if we looked at it only at the moment of placing it in the water or for a few minutes afterward, we might not believe that it was going to dissolve. Time is the frame of reference in which transformation occurs, and what becomes transformed are the illusions about who we are, into the truth of our being.

On the level of thoughts and wishes, time is the medium in which our wishes take form and unfold before us. In this same way does a seed become a plant, an acorn become a tree, and a thought become a reality. The principle of Spirit releasing energy through thought and becoming form holds true in all cases, and it is only within a narrow view of time that we are deceived into believing that the seed will not grow or that our wishes will not manifest.

Time is not our enemy. It allows, through its *neutrality*, the force of our creative inner impulse—our will-power—to push its way forward and to work with the operating laws of the Universe, of evolution, of karma, and of manifestation. Time is the neutral medium in which our will expresses, and this will can reflect the desires of the unconscious, conscious, or superconscious mind.

The unconscious mind, as we have said, is connected with the desire to fulfill emotional needs; the conscious mind has as its content whatever we are aware of in our mental process; the superconscious mind is the voice of our Soul, whose purpose is to further our growth on spiritual levels. When we do not see something manifesting as quickly as we would like in life, it may not be because there is anything *wrong* with the energy we are sending out; it may be that that energy has not been fully integrated with the energy of our Soul's purpose, and that our conscious and superconscious minds are *in conflict* about what is desirable. More and more, as we integrate mind, body, and Spirit, we allow our Soul or higher Self to speak through us and to express itself in our lives. As this happens, the source of the creative energy flow into the Universe—the *source* of our will-power—shifts from our personality and conscious mind to our superconscious mind and Soul.

Therefore, Beloveds, let us determine that when we become discouraged about not having what we wish, we will look closely to see *from which part of ourselves* we are sending forth our intentions. It may be that what we wish for is *less than what we are meant to have*, and that if we could only wait, we would see that our Soul at the very moment of our experiencing conflict and deprivation, was working toward the fulfillment of our highest goals, rather than the fulfillment of lesser goals that were easier to achieve.

Beloveds, patience and humility before the creative power of the Soul and a willingness to let it do its work are necessary on the spiritual path. And we must become clearer as we work with our higher creative power, to see if we are expressing the highest goals we are capable of manifesting. When we aim for the highest, we can know that what we wish for will ultimately materialize in the medium of time and space, for it is one with our deepest purpose and one with our heart's desire.

PAX

To give ourselves permission to live a life in which we do what "feels right", is to sanction our Soul's jurisdiction over the material world. It is to assign greater weight to the spiritual power that moves through our lives than to the physical forces that have held authority over our actions.

Chapter 29

The Soul's Purpose in Life

We are at a crossroad in consciousness, Beloveds, where what we do and what we are can be fully penetrated by our Soul's purpose, or we can choose to continue to travel through the world embodying the desires of the physical and the sensate. Each one of us must make this choice, and in choosing, we determine both our individual fate and the destiny of the planet.

We have come far in our spiritual development, far enough for our minds to know what our souls intend, and if we choose, our actions can express what is linked to both mind *and* spirit. For many of us this level of spiritual integration was not possible before now, and the few who achieved it in our historical past were often leaders of mankind. Yet the present is a time of revelation, Beloveds—a time of greater energy moving through the Earth plane; this enables the mind to more easily make contact with the voice of Spirit.

As we look into our hearts in the present moment, we must ask ourselves which direction our present motives lead us in—toward the satisfaction of material desire, or the satisfaction of spiritual longing or a combination of the two. For the desire to live according to our soul's purpose must be a pure one, sincerely felt, not one that becomes a new label for us to pin on our psyches. The Soul, guardian of our passage through the Earth plane, has watched our progress for countless incarnations, waiting for the time when we would awaken to its presence. Now, at this time, we can begin to feel its energy surging through us, as we increasingly feel the call to realize our deepest nature.

Beloveds, each lifetime is given over to a specific area of development and growth which brings into the foreground of our awareness qualities of mind and spirit that have been less available to us in previous incarnations. Yet viewed from the perspective of the Eternal, within each lifetime we are simply manifesting a different facet of the Divine spark that we are, always seeking greater consciousness of ourselves *as* that spark, and learning simultaneously to relate to the divinity within all others.

We have chosen to incarnate on the Earth plane to fully express our Soul's purpose, and each incarnation has its own specific goals in this regard. It may be to develop a sense of personal power or will, or to realize a deeper understanding of love, or to develop the potential of the mind through scientific work or artistic creation, or to understand the relationship between the individual consciousness and the universal consciousness—the "I" and the "Self." All of these goals are fundamentally spiritual, though they may be manifested in lives that do not overtly reflect their spiritual quality.

Each life, no matter what the occupation or interest of the being who has incarnated, has a fundamentally spiritual purpose and aim, often unknown to the one who is simply experiencing it on the physical plane.

The aim provides the driving force or motivation for the successive challenges, life- crises, or issues that that individual will face over the entire lifetime.

Looked at from the perspective of the Soul, each phase of a life can be viewed in terms of its furthering the development of the Soul's purpose. During each part, we are driven onward by that force or interest which gives greatest *meaning* to our lives, and this is what we focus on, attend to, and devote our energy to. It is precisely this search for the meaningful throughout a lifetime that carries with it the fulfillment of the Soul's purpose.

Beloveds, lessons that seem to be psychological in nature, for instance those that are involved in relationships to others, whether painful or joyful, always have this transcendent quality of meaning. Significant relationships teach us something about who we are *in our souls*, and give us a heightened awareness of our individuality and being-ness. Any relationship, situation or experience that assists us in becoming more aware of our being-ness—that which exists at the core of "I Am"—has been brought into our lives from the soul level in order to further our self-consciousness as Divine beings. Raising children has this effect, as does pursuing specific academic, professional, or financial goals.

Being attuned to nature and the outdoors speaks to us of our innermost being, as does reading certain books, or hearing certain pieces of music. If we could be more sensitive to the slight shifts in consciousness that occur within us as we experience, we would see that each moment we live changes our self-awareness and self-perception to some degree. The magical moments of life, those that we consciously experience as transformative, change our self-perception most of all.

The learning that is necessary in order to make the shift from a physical or psychological interpretation of events to a spiritual one, requires a willingness within us to trust our intuitive sense of the meaningful—to notice when we seem especially to respond to something with a heightened sense of alertness, presentness, and interest. This "presentness" can take place in relation to a color, a song, a smell, a person that we know, a quality of interaction, a subject of interest, an activity, a view of the sky or of the sea. The indication of our Soul's presence is to be found in the *energized quality of perception* which exists at certain moments of life, that gives to that perception a heightened sense of reality, even when the precise meaning of that moment or experience is not consciously understood. When we follow this perceptual guide, we can see where our lives are headed, by looking at the flow of energy that exists in the *now*.

What do we find really engrossing to do, to feel, to think about? What captures our attention, our imagination, our love? At certain points in a life it may be that the soul's learning comes through a small door or opening in physical reality, and that only one or two things will be of heightened interest. This is especially true when a love relationship is flowering, and the quality of lovingness for a while becomes the all-absorbing center of the soul's learning. Or, to take another example, in the case of pain or illness, the individual for longer or shorter periods may be totally focused on his relationship to the pain and to the body; at that time *this* relationship becomes the true source of the soul's learning. More often, however, our soul is capable of learning from many different events and experiences, and that learning is accelerated by our *willingness to become conscious* of ourselves and our perceptions.

This willingness to become conscious, Beloveds, takes place when we have developed a sufficient degree of personality integration so that we *know* what it is that we really like, and what we feel "drawn to." There is a time before this knowing occurs, however when the personality is not fully formed, when the individual does not separate herself much from the collective consciousness, and the root of her individuality and selfhood is therefore not perceived. When personality integration reaches a certain level of attainment, then the subtleties of tastes, preferences , attractions, repulsions, etc. become clearer, and we have the opportunity of becoming more deeply involved in the adventure which is our life.

As we notice ourselves becoming attracted to a particular person or event, even to a kind of food or a kind of movie, we can comprehend the spiritual meaning of this experience by allowing ourselves to fully engage with it— to taste it, to see what we like about it, to permit ourselves the inner flowering that is possible when an activity is energized by its connection with our Soul's purpose. This attunement and attention not only creates greater interest for us in our life-experiences, but also facilitates the integration of the new learning itself. Attention, dear ones, is the critical key: to pay attention to our experience at all times—to validate it at all times—this is what living a spiritual life is about. It is a life which honors our priceless selfhood with a determination to more deeply penetrate the mysteries of inner being.

It is not necessary to sit and meditate for long periods of time in order to develop this perception of "I-ness"; meditation creates but one dimension or frame in which to view the "I" that is our center. Within daily life as well, we can choose to recognize the movements, directions and yearnings, that bring us into a state of greater alertness, and those that take us into a state of greater withdrawal and listlessness. What is key is the quality of *relatedness* between the "I" that is experiencing and what is being experienced.

Television, for example, often arouses great interest within us and we attend well. Yet most often there is no conscious relationship between the perceiver and that which is perceived. It is instead an experience of abandoning self-consciousness and awareness, not of going more deeply into it.

When we attune to our Soul's desire for us, we can simply sit quietly for a moment and ask what it is we are meant to be doing right now. The answer that comes is often not in words, but rather in terms of something that *feels right*. This quality of "feeling right" must be taken quite seriously, for it is our intuitive guide to the path of inner guidance; it is the clue that we are being led into a state of greater harmony with our own Divine plan, and with the will of our higher Self. This attunement to the feeling-quality of a situation, Beloveds, can become a new way of life for us—one in which we experience the self as perpetually expanding in newness and in joy. To give ourselves permission to live a life where we do what "feels right", is to sanction our Soul's jurisdiction over the material world. It is to assign greater weight to the spiritual power that moves through our lives than to the physical forces that have held authority over our actions.

This is the choice we must make, Beloveds, and we make it at every moment of deciding. In one direction we choose the goal of retaining the approval of the world with its structures and authorities, its ways of validating us from an economic, social, aesthetic, or emotional point of view. In the other direction we choose the authority of the Soul, which speaks through the flow of energy that is increasingly available to us and perceivable by us if we attend to it.

We are at a crossroad, Beloveds, and we cannot go in both directions at the same time. Let us ask for guidance that our minds and hearts may be opened to the highest Truth for each of us. May we learn to dwell in the land of courage, honesty, and compassion, allowing all others to go a different way from our way, while knowing that *our* way, our path, is the only one that is possible for *us* to follow.

PAX

You who would climb the mountain to the fire of Heaven must know that the rod of Abraham is given to those who have proven their courage to stand in the flame of annihilation, through continuing attitudes of selflessness within waking and sleeping life, within meditation and dream life, at all times, and in all levels of awareness.

Chapter 30

The Dreamscape

Within the far reaches of the mind there is a fire burning—a fire of creativity and power so great that it can illuminate the world. No one tends this fire, for it is the self-generated AUM at the core of the Universe and at the core of individual creation. This fire burns hotly at all times, giving off heat which turns into imagination, volition, character, motivation, and reasoning—each process given life by this flame of the Divine. The fire is the source of the Godhead—the fountain from which springs all being, and each of us must turn toward it to replenish our resources when we are tired, and to search for inspiration when we feel empty. The fire of the Godhead *is* the Burning Bush: The image that Moses saw but a reflection of it, for it burns a thousand times more brightly than the solar radiance the human eye is accustomed to beholding. Therefore in ancient times, the wise ones were instructed not to look at the ark of the covenant, which contained within itself the fire of God, for without adequate preparation they would have been blinded.

The energy vortex emerging from this primordial fire is like lightning, bringing to the air an electrical discharge of release, which breaks open the sanctimonious concepts of reason that a new vision may be created within the minds of men. It is the vision of the reality of God, whose power fertilizes all sacred ground with this primordial energy, within the galaxy, within the solar system, within the Earth, and within the human being.

There is no state more terrible to realize than that in which one feels cut off from the Father-Mother Sprit—the flame of Creation—the Godhead. Yet whether we see it or not, the burning goes on and on, within the Universe and within our immortal Spirit, endlessly creating newness, endlessly spinning out of It's holy Self visions of immortality that once created, exist for all time. These visions are inalterably linked to the Being that is God, Who shall always remain nameless. For to name the existence of the Godhead is to refer to only the merest shadow and fraction of that creative power burning at the heart of the Universe.

Generations may come and go, but the flame of the Divine burns unceasingly, unfailingly, allowing the vision of God to manifest within the finite world. This fire is the source of the Divine breath, which breathes through all of life, the source of in-spiration and of Truth. There can be no question that its justice and mercy are inextricably part of its essence; otherwise its flames would sear and destroy that which it created. Yet what is created once can never be destroyed, but rather lives for eternity within the Divine flame.

Molten lava flows from the cave at the entrance to the temple housing the Divine flame, and none can approach it who have not first been bathed in the waters of purification and annihilation, who, through adherence to the faith of the elders, learn the way of approach without being burned before this entrance. Self-annihilation is mandatory for such a one, since the self, as humans know it, is merely a sophistry, a construction of the lower mind and imagination, having little to do with the real essence of oneness and divinity that is the true being. *To behold the majesty of the Divine fire, one must walk clothed only in the garments of the Soul; there is no other path of approach. For the Divine cannot be in the presence of that which is not Divine—that which is not fully purified in the furnace of Love.*

The rod of Abraham gave to certain ones in that generation the power to behold the face of the Divine in the sense that I now speak of it. This rod, though lost in its physical form, has been passed down to the elders of each generation, that those who seek in truth shall find the catalyzing energy of that rod within their human experience. The rod of Abraham is not a metaphor, but a real instrument for transferring the energy of the Godhead through the physical plane, so that the consciousness of one who is becoming one with his own Soul can attain entrance to the heart of God.

Seek not to display works of devotion or words of selflessness, or to place much emphasis on the quality of meditation that brings you into a state of peace and harmony as it in-spires you with more of the Divine breath. All these are useful, but they do not in themselves provide access to the Fire of God—to the face of God.

You who would climb the mountain to the fire of Heaven must know that the rod of Abraham is given to those who have proven their courage to stand in the flame of annihilation, through continuing attitudes of selflessness within waking and sleeping life, within meditation and dream life, at all times, and in all levels of awareness.

This self-abnegation is the single most important factor enabling one to stand before the throne of the Holy of Holies, and to look upon the face of the Beloved. For unless one has lost the self, there can be no appreciation of what is not the Other, but oneself also, in a far truer sense.

The unity of self with Self takes place on the highest planes of consciousness that man can attain, and it is there that the crown is placed on the head of one who has for so long struggled to attain this moment of contact. The crown of victory is given to that one who struggles, generation after generation and life after life, to bring purity, selflessness, and total love for God's creatures into his life, to destroy the illusion of the lower self, and to bring forth the strength and capacity necessary to receive Divine illumination.

This is not a matter of the work done in one lifetime alone, but of work done on a soul level through countless lifetimes, little by little breaking down the illusions of the false-self, so that that which is true and only that can be seen through the veil of illusion.

There can be no victory for one who does not possess the temperament of the stalwart, of the victorious conqueror or as it was called "the overcomer." For such a one has become inured to the trials of life, recognizing that these trials are but stepping stones to the citadel which contains the temple of the Most High. Strength at all times, to continue onward toward one's destination, releasing self, abandoning the path of mortality and of fear, absolutely abandoning oneself to the faith that only one's Divine Self is real—this is what is needed.

This kind of strength can only be found by those who tread the path of initiation, and once acquired, it can never be lost. For the way to the Godhead is marked by certain stations, and once having passed any of these there is no turning back to a lesser state of awareness. This is not desired, nor is it possible, for the victory of Truth over illusion cannot be undone, even if it be undone temporarily, and he who walks alone up the mountain path toward the Burning Bush cannot choose another hill that would satisfy the need to see God face to face. There is no other hill for that one, nor can there be another answer to his seeking. For such a one the journey of climbing forever upward is the only journey to take, and no matter what pain or difficulty may occur along the way, that one will not be deterred. For the lesser self is already dying, and only the light of the fire of the Divine has an importance on this path. Only the hope of seeing the face of God has any meaning, and all else pales by comparison.

Pain and pleasure, sadness and grief, success and failure may all come to one who seeks the path of Glory, but these will appear as insignificant. What matters is only that which brings one before the throne where the crowning of the Soul takes place. This truth burns in the heart of those who seek this path, and that inner fire is only an ember of the Divine flame that shall burn when the seeker becomes one with that which is sought, and the lesser fire becomes unified with the greater.

Therefore do not lose heart in journeying to Truth, for the only reality lies before you, and that which you have left behind shall soon dry up and disappear as the ashes that remain after a fire has been extinguished. There shall be no more grief as the real becomes more real, and separates itself from what has been only an illusion. And this in truth is the destiny for those who seek the flame of the Divine, the face of God. That victory shall be theirs, and all that they hope for shall be realized.

PAX

This is a glorious time in history, Beloveds, and we are both witnesses and participants in the awakening of the planetary Spirit. As the earth awakens we awaken as well, for our consciousness is shared, and the energy moves back and forth. And what we awaken to, dear ones, is our position of stewardship here, to our connection with all forms of life, and in beginning to live this truth do we each become saviours of the Earth.

Chapter 31

Saviors of the World

Dear ones, there is within each heart a sacred space consecrated to the development of the universal Soul. This space has been kept hidden from all but the most exalted eyes, for to see the universal Soul—the soul of the Earth—is to know God as well. We are not ultimately merely individuals leading separate lives on this verdant planet. We are that too, but we are much, much more. Like the cells of a body of any organism, we are part of a greater Life whose consciousness is composed of the many individual consciousnesses that we each are. This One, that has been called the "planetary Logos," is the One Who from the beginning of the creation of the Earth has waited patiently within the Earthsphere for consciousness to awaken within itself. We, the individual identities that recognize ourselves as Divine, *are* that awakening consciousness, and as each of us awakens to our divinity, so too does the Earth awaken on a far grander scale.

We are the crystals or lenses which focus and transmit light between the Earth and the cosmos, and in doing so we create alignment and attunement between the two. We are the bridge upon which the Earth and the cosmic Spirit become joined in holy matrimony. We humankind, have inherited the sacred task of joining Matter and Spirit within our own consciousness, and we do this at every moment through our every thought and action.

We must not underestimate the importance of the role we play in the life of the Earth, for we are the connecting link between sub-systems. We are the brain sending messages to those lesser forms of life within the planetary body that rely on human action for their maintenance and sustenance. We are also the transmitters of Earth's energy to the Universe, and we announce now that we are ready to receive the impulses coming from the cosmic Spirit which will fully awaken the planet through us—the lenses, the channels, they transmitters of the sacred Word.

This is the meaning of the Son-ship, Beloveds, and it is time for us to honor the role we have chosen as bridge between Spirit and Matter, between Heaven and Earth. Each of us can choose to contribute to the task of preserving, expanding, sanctifying, and initiating the Earth into full awareness of Her part in the cosmic harmonies. Yet whether or not we choose to lead responsible lives as conscious stewards of this planet, *the Earth will awaken*, for Her time has come, and "the turtle doves are upon the land." The Earth *will* awaken, and we, depending on our openness to change, will experience that awakening with Her, as the cosmic current streams ever more strongly to us and through us.

This is a glorious time in history, Beloveds, and we are both witnesses and participants in the awakening of the planetary Spirit. As the Earth awakens we awaken as well, for our consciousness is shared, and the energy moves back and forth. What we awaken to, dear ones, is our position of stewardship here, to our connection with all forms of life, and in beginning to live this truth do we each become saviours of the Earth.

Native Americans and other ancient peoples have known this truth for thousands of years. In their devotion to the sacred land and their preservation of a sacred relationship with animals, they have anchored this understanding for all of us.

Yet now, humankind as a whole is beginning to realize that the task just before us is to generate an unequalled force for peace, light, and the purposes of Spirit. Now we must begin to transform the energies coming to us into actions that will aid the life of the Earth, and help Her expand into greater awareness.

Beloveds, the practice of stewardship is simple and can be expressed in the simplest of gestures. We must consciously preserve life, not alienate it—whether that be the life of a stream or river, of the forests, or of other humans. We are each responsible for the preservation of life as just stewards of the world. Wherever we see the impulse arising within ourselves to take life lightly, from the smallest of insects to the largest of trees—we must remind ourselves that all life holds consciousness, and all consciousness contributes to the consciousness of the one Soul of which we are a part. Therefore we must act with respect for the sacredness of each, and in acting, acknowledge the trust that we have been given.

To become a saviour of the world is the destiny of each of us, Beloveds, a destiny that we chose before the beginning of our incarnationsl cycle; it is only a matter of time before each of us recognizes our responsibility toward one another, in word as well as in deed. We are responsible because together we form a collective vibration or Soul which affects each and every living thing on the planet, and within the Universe as well. And we are responsible to the Mother that has given birth to us and carried us within her nest-body, Who now asks that we honor the greater consciousness of which we are a part, and which forms part of us.

There is no ultimate separation, Beloveds, between the consciousness of the planet and our own consciousness.

All thoughts form one common pathway of thought. All lives influence our own. Yet just as parts of our physical body become differentiated in terms of form and function—some having greater responsibility for the organism's functioning than others, some having greater sensitivity to receive messages than others—so too do we have the possiblity of developing ourselves to the highest degree we choose, so that we may manifest the highest and purest level of the Divine pattern that we reflect and that we are.

This choice belongs to each of us, and we make it all the time, with each thought that we think and with each breath we take.

Dear ones, the stage is set for the next act of the historical drama and it will unfold before us, within us, and around us. We have so much to share with others—with other humans and with other life-forms. Indeed, we are looked at with awe and admiration by celestial beings that watch the Earth, for the role we have chosen to play is a complex and sacred one. We have agreed to develop our awareness and the use of our will to achieve universal aims, and we are being asked to dedicate body, mind, and spirit toward the furthering of these aims.

The time is *now*, Beloveds, at this most amazing moment in history, to fully accept our responsibility as saviours of the world, and to know that we are one Soul, one Life, one Breath. In doing this, our Souls will rejoice and our hearts will sing as we recognize our participation in the universal.

And the song upon our lips will be the song of humanity that lived and died striving to bring the ideal of universal brother-sisterhood into being upon the Earth. And the song will be the song of Spirit, rejoicing as hearts open to the wonder of this truth whose realization is just upon the horizon.

Can you see it now, Beloveds? It is just before us lighting up the sky with a new sunrise of hope. Can you see it shining there?

It is a prayer for a new day, spoken in the voice of tomorrow:

"May God bless us and keep us within the sacredness of His presence. From this day forward may we experience the holiness of Spirit within the temple of Matter in which we live, to give and receive Thy blessings . . . Beloved."

PAX

A
Uni★Sun
BOOK

Books and Products to help establish
The Global Spiritual Awakening

Julie Redstone is a bright new star in Uni★Sun's constellation of writers. She is a healer and clinical psychologist transformed in 1982 following a dramatic spiritual awakening. She lives and works in Amherst, Massachusetts, and is Director of the Amherst Center for Healing.

We at Uni★Sun are happy and proud to publish books and offer products that make a real contribution to the global spiritual awakening already begun on this planet. Julie Redstone is one of several important new authors whose work we publish. Please write for our free catalogue.

UNI★SUN
P.O. Box 25421
Kansas City, MO 64119
U.S.A.